Something aw
Something awesome is going to happen today!
Something awesome is going to happen today!

EXPECTING
AWESOME
DAILY

ROB VIVIAN

EXECTING AWESOME DAILY
Copyright (c) 2019 by Rob Vivian

All rights reserved. No part of this book may be used or reproduced by any means, graphic, electronic, or mechanical, including photocopying, recording, taping or by any information storage retrieval system without the written permission of the author except in the case of brief quotations embodied in critical articles and reviews.

ISBN: 978-1-77374-050-8 (Print)
ISBN: 978-1-77374-051-5 (Ebook)

Typeset and cover design by Edge of Water Designs, edgeofwater.com

Printed in Canada

OTHER BOOKS BY THE AUTHOR

The Grass is Greener on This Side of the Fence

The Realtor's Magic Formula

Success Explosion

ACKNOWLEDGEMENTS

Being in a position to write several books would not be possible without the help of all the important people in my life. It really is difficult to name everyone, as there are so many.

My parents, Fran and Norm, have had the greatest influence on my life by teaching me a wide range of life skills. My wife of almost 36 years, Coleen, is the person who keeps me grounded, as my mind is prone to wander.

My children, Josh and Corissa, are really awesome, and play instrumental, ongoing roles in our company, "Rob Vivian Coaching." My siblings Norma, Randy, Rick, and Eric always have my back, which is comforting for me.

Last, but certainly not least, I sincerely thank God for all my blessings: I definitely have much more than I deserve!

DEDICATION

*I would like to dedicate this book
to my brother, Randy,
who passed away suddenly
during the later stages
of the writing of this book.*

Randy Thomas Vivian 1958 – 2019

EXPECTING
AWESOME
DAILY

ROB VIVIAN

TABLE OF CONTENTS

Acknowledgements 5

Dedication 7

For Starters 13

Chapter One: Your Life's Journey 17

Chapter Two: Everybody Qualifies 34

Chapter Three: Now Is the Time 43

Chapter Four: Perspective is Everything 57

Chapter Five: Yes You Can 73

Chapter Six: Don't Be Your Own Obstacle 89

Chapter Seven: Control What You Can 103

Chapter Eight: Embrace 117

Chapter Nine: What Do You Have? 133

Chapter Ten: Fire Up the Rocket 142

Final Thoughts 153

Notes 155

FOR STARTERS

THE PURPOSE OF this book is to assist the reader in achieving a certain state of mind: to live each and every day with an unconditional expectation that something awesome is going to happen today. To spend our days fully *Expecting Awesome Daily*. Life is busy, and more often than not resembles a full-contact sport—and I am here to suggest that this is good news.

Hockey is my favourite sport. I love playing the game and following my (often frustrating) team, the Toronto Maple Leafs. Some games are low-key: a bit of a defensive match without much happening. In the end, we're happy if our team comes out on top.

Other times, the game takes on a much different tone: intense, end-to-end action, it leaves us holding our breath and sitting on the edge of our seats. In the end—win, lose, or draw—we experienced an amazing game.

If you were asked to choose which you'd prefer to be involved in, it goes without saying that you would pick the latter every time. The thrill of the wild ride would be everyone's choice. Life is like that, and you should want that.

For Starters

At the end of your days, I hope you can say that you purposefully experienced the thrills of the wild ride: a sense of accomplishment, combined with some disappointments, but quickly followed by another thrilling achievement. That's life; that's the ideal design. Embrace it and maximize your experiences.

You will never feel more alive than the few minutes after an intense roller coaster ride, so intentionally live your life that way. If you are at the amusement park with children, of course you take them on the kiddie rides; however, you are not a child, so don't go living your life that way. Your life should resemble the thrill of the wild ride.

As you experience the natural ups and downs that make up this amazing thing we call life, it's easy to lose our focus. We must deliberately train our brain to exist in a place where *Expecting Awesome Daily* is our normal train of thought.

My attempt in this book is to shine a light on the aspects of your life that effectively block your ability to live in the mental state of *Expecting Awesome Daily*. This will, in turn, give you some ammunition to combat the enemies of complacency, procrastination, and unnecessary fear that currently stand in your way of experiencing life on the adult ride.

There is a reason kiddie rides are called what they are: they are made for kids. I realize that they are safe, while the adult rides do possess some risk; however, you must know in your heart that you are made to live in the adult world.

I'm not saying that this book makes you a whole person: please understand this. This book is designed to assist you towards living in a state of mind that is on the lookout for awesome events on a daily basis. It is the state of mind that I, personally, think is the optimal state required for an amazing life.

Some would say that other aspects of your life are far more important than your daily mindset. For instance, many would say that your spiritual position is more important than a positive mindset; I happen to agree. As a spiritual person myself, I acknowledge that this book is certainly further down the list of life's important lessons. Will I write some spiritual books in the future? Perhaps. However, for now my goal is to assist you in improving your daily attitude and mindset.

To accomplish this, I have inserted a helpful exercise at the end of each chapter. I realize that many of us do not like to complete such exercises inside of a book itself to guard against others seeing our innermost thoughts, challenges, and struggles. However, it is important that the exercises are completed. Perhaps you can complete them outside the book, or at the very least spend a few minutes in thought prior to proceeding to the next chapter.

Life is going by: grab hold of it and never, under any circumstances, let go. There is always the option to play it small: to spend your days on the kiddie rides or even to sit on a bench watching others experience the thrill of life's amazing wild rides.

Living in a state of *Expecting Awesome Daily* will go a long way to getting you on the correct ride.

Enjoy!

Something awesome is going to happen today!

Rob Vivian

Chapter One

YOUR LIFE'S JOURNEY

IT'S BEEN SAID that the journey is as much fun as the destination. The concept being that enjoyment, value, and fulfilment can and will be experienced along the way. This is in opposition to the concept of "put your head down and work hard" towards a perceived payoff at some point in the future. If you take the time to evaluate these processes in advance, consider the two options carefully:

Option #1

Put your head down, sacrifice, and push yourself toward your desired result. You will experience your reward at some point in the future. Unfortunately, the catch to this method is that your entire reward is held back to be given on a future date. It can therefore be difficult to persevere on a daily basis, since no reward is available to act as incentive along the way.

Option #2

As you work toward your ultimate goal, smaller achievements are accomplished. These small rewards inject motivation into your process as you travel down your chosen path.

Option #1 is the one which I can confidently say that most choose. Unfortunately, the journey isn't as much fun as the destination with that method: all of the reward is withheld until the desired goal is achieved. Option #2 permits portions of the reward to be achieved along the way, allowing the success of the journey to match that of the destination.

In both cases the rewards are probably equal. In Option #1, 100% of the payoff is experienced upon the completion of the goal. In Option #2, only a smaller payoff is held back, since a portion is experienced as you travel toward your goal. You do possess the right to select the path: both Option #1 and Option #2 are available to you.

So, for the next goal you set, consider yourself to be at a crossroads. You will be standing at a fork in the road with two road signs. The sign pointing to the left says: Your Goal This Way. And beneath it: 50% Enjoyed Along the Way, 50% Enjoyed Upon Completion.

The sign pointing to the right says the same thing: Your Goal This Way. However, beneath this sign it reads: 100% Enjoyed Upon Completion.

This book is called *Expecting Awesome Daily*. It's about living every day with the expectation that something awesome is going to happen. Let's consider your frame of mind if you mistakenly choose Option #1 as your desired route. On that road, your head is down, the blinders are on, and you are mustering all your energy to propel yourself toward your worthwhile goal.

I think you would agree that, in this state, you are not allowing space for an awesome event to enter your life; in fact, it's quite likely that if something awesome did try to present itself to you, it would go unnoticed in your head-down mindset.

On the other hand, let's consider Option #2. You have embarked on a worthwhile goal in whatever aspect of your life you deem important; or perhaps you have such a goal in all the aspects of your life—which, of course, would be a great idea. As you travel, you are fully aware that you have chosen the route where the journey is as much fun as the destination. You are expecting to experience 50% of the benefit along the way and pick up the remainder upon completion.

In this scenario, your head is not mentally down—in fact, quite the opposite. You are like a hawk, constantly looking around and noticing everything. You ask yourself, "Is this the day that a portion of my reward will come my way?" You are purposefully living with the expectation that something awesome is going to happen today.

Let's take a look at an example to drive this point home. Although goals could, and should, be set in all aspects of your life (be it financial, spiritual, health, family, or friends), for ease of use I'm going to use a financial goal as an example. Let's pretend that, somehow, you have found yourself with $25,000 of stressful, unwanted debt. I'm referring to bad debt here, from something like credit cards.

You could choose Option #1: to mentally put your head down and work single-mindedly to eliminate the debt. Depending on your income, this could happen relatively quickly or require several years. Either way, as you work toward the elimination of a debt that has probably weighed on you, I feel that your mindset would be somewhat closed. You know in your mind that the relief of this debt all comes at the end.

With this option, I would be concerned about your enjoyment of life (or the lack thereof) as you travel toward this worthwhile goal. I think you would agree that your daily mindset would be something less than *Expecting Awesome Daily*.

On the other hand, let's consider Option #2. There is no doubt that the $25,000 debt must be eliminated; let's agree that, in your case, two years will be allocated. In Option #2, we need to build in some benefit along the way to make the journey as much fun as the destination. So let's plan a little celebration every $5,000: something to mark the completion of the first leg of your journey. Obviously a $5,000 trip would be counterproductive. The reward doesn't need to be something extravagant, just an acknowledgment.

I would recommend something in the $200 range: large enough that it's enjoyable, but not so large as to set you back. If you are a golfer, perhaps a round at a course that you wouldn't normally play; if food is your thing, a nice dinner out; if you prefer to sit back, perhaps a relaxing spa day; you get the picture.

The idea is to enjoy your journey: to expect awesome things to happen every day. Your mindset will be much better if, mentally, your head is up and looking around, rather than committing several years to putting your head down for enjoyment at some point in the future.

I hope that you and I live to a ripe old age; however, you know that is not guaranteed. What is guaranteed is today. It's good to have goals: just choose fulfilment along the way, and cash in on the final balance upon completion.

Path Less Travelled

Seeing as most people fail in their quest for greatness, or even their smaller, worthwhile goals, it would be a good idea to purposefully choose not to follow those that are destined to fail.

However, there is no doubt that the path less travelled can, at times, be challenging. Consider, for example, a national park: a lot of time and resources are spent on the paths commonly travelled. They are smoother, wider, and probably meticulously groomed. Of course, it does make sense to pay more attention to the paths that see more foot traffic. But for those that seek real adventure, exploring the lesser-used paths could be exciting. Or maybe you could even consider blazing your own trail.

If you are looking for real adventure and fulfillment, get off the beaten path. Go your own way, be that on a path less travelled or on a new path you are the creator of. We must consciously choose to veer off the beaten path to one that fewer people find interesting or have the courage to discover.

Always choosing the path less travelled on purpose will separate you from the masses who often fail. I'm not saying there won't be danger: perhaps a financial challenge lies along that less-travelled trail. In actuality, most of those who succeed do experience some financial strain in the beginning—but they press on. Maybe it's that a relationship no longer has interest for you in your off-the-beaten-path attitude. There will be challenges; however, they are surmountable, unlike a real forest walk, where a bear or cougar may lurk.

If it helps, think about a gold miner back in the day of prospecting. If he chooses to take the well-travelled path and mine where many others are mining, for sure, he can find some gold. However, don't you think it would be a much better idea if he went to a different location? If he took the risk and discovered his own mine?

I'm sure many gold prospectors played it safe. They took the road commonly travelled and spent their time mining with the others. I don't think those were the ones that made their fortunes, though; fortunes were achieved by those who had the courage to go their own way—to break away from the crowd and blaze a new trail.

Seeing as the vast majority of people fail, the process becomes quite simple: watch what others are doing—the commonly travelled path—and do the opposite—the path less travelled.

Take Stock

Most people are too hard on themselves, which, of course, hinders the process of having awesome things happen to them every day. The secret is to take stock of what you have. You are not starting from zero. However, if you are too hard on yourself, it will feel like that is precisely the case.

I have many conversations with our clients daily. Overall, they are doing amazing, and they call me periodically to share their amazing news. However, most of the calls I receive are on the subject of needing advice to overcome a challenge that lies in their path.

I start by asking questions: what do we have or possess that could be beneficial in resolving this unwanted obstacle? What's interesting is that most of the time I am required to dig it out of them.

I listen to the challenge, then say, "Okay, what do we have now?

What skills do we possess that we could leverage and be helpful?" The most common response is, "I got nothing." At that point, I inform them that they are being way too hard on themselves. They do have some skills, and they do have some knowledge. All we have to do is access it.

It's true that, in some situations, the phrase "I got nothing" would be correct. In the beginning, for instance, when a concept is brand-new to you, you would not possess any reference points to start from. Everything you need to learn is currently in the unlearned category.

However, if you are anywhere down the road of accomplishment and were to claim "I got nothing," a wise instructor would say, "That's not true; let's think it through and assist you in accessing the knowledge you do possess, even if it's not complete."

In our journey through life, the situation where our knowledge and skill level are 100% absent is the rare one. Even when we embark on a quest to discover a new, less travelled path, we often do in fact possess some ability we can access, be it a partial skill or some knowledge.

The point I'm making here is that far too often we quickly fall to the assumption of "I got nothing." That's not helpful. You are more talented than you give yourself credit for: you contain so much more than is visible on the surface. Get into the habit of taking stock when obstacles or challenges present themselves, and veer away from the defeatist "I got nothing" mindset. You are smarter, stronger, and possess far more abilities than you give yourself credit for.

If you train yourself to automatically search for what weapons you have in your arsenal, you are training yourself to be a solution-driven person. If, on the other hand, you too quickly assume "I got nothing," you are unfortunately conditioning yourself to be a problem-driven person.

You have a choice, and I would highly recommend you choose to become a solution-driven person. You are going to need this skill as you journey down the path less travelled.

Limit Worry

I suppose "eliminate worry" would be better; however, I'm not sure that is achievable. It's easy to say, but quite another thing to accomplish. Personally, I'm a person who doesn't worry much. Having said that, even I worry sometimes about different aspects of my life. I could honestly say that this amount is minimal; overall, I'm not a worrier, and so this is not one of the qualities I'm looking to improve.

If you are like me and worry just isn't something that plagues you on a regular basis, that's convenient. However, if worry is a challenge for you, I recommend you pay close attention.

Now, I love action movies. In order for an action movie to possess a plot, you need a hero and a villain. Your brain is like that: either it's your hero or it's your villain. If your thinking is predominately positive, consciously focussing on life-building categories, then your brain is your hero. Characteristics in this category are items like gratitude, contribution, looking on the bright side, and dozens of other positive attributes.

However, even as positive as you are, you may have accidently invited negative characteristics to make a home in your brain. If too many of these unwanted visitors take up residence, your brain instead becomes your villain. Attributes that fall into this category include items like envy, self-centeredness, and, among others, worry.

There are some negative qualities that, although harmful overall, can produce some benefit. As an example, let's take a look at greed. A bad quality to possess, greed will create a lasting, negative impact on your life and that of those around you. As harmful as that is, because of greed you would probably be driven to accomplish more. That, in turn, might even supply a quality lifestyle for your family—at least from a financial point of view.

Let me be clear: the negative impact of greed far outweighs the positive. However, it would be unfair to pretend that a positive aspect does not exist.

Worry is not like that. All the ramifications of worry are on the negative side of the ledger. It's a well-documented fact that worry can, and will, cause all sorts of physical ailments: some of which are fatal.

This book, *Expecting Awesome Daily*, is going to require your hero-brain, not the villain-brain that dominates the vast majority of Earth's residents. Worry is an awesome killer.

Life is full of choices, so don't kid yourself. You can make a conscious decision to either be a person who is plagued with worry or a person who, like me, only worries periodically. Never allow worry the opportunity to become one of your defining characteristics.

I personally know some people who have allowed worry to become one of their defining characteristics, as I'm sure you do as well. Some of these individuals have been a part of my life for many years. Although I love them dearly, no one is looking to them for inspiration. They are not, and never will be, the patriarchs: their continual worry has created an aura of negativity over time. It's very unhealthy: physically, mentally, and pretty much on every level. I hope this person I'm describing isn't you; if it is, take action immediately. Excessive worry leads to cynicism, and who wants to be around that?

In order to live your days honestly expecting something awesome to happen, you have to think about travelling through your day on the lookout for that awesome something. Think about your state of mind: excited, happy, fun. The type of person everyone wants to be around. If you are a business person, this is an ideal personality type: every potential customer who meets you will pick up on your positive vibe. Everyone wants to be a part of that.

They say that the majority of what we worry about never happens; I fully agree with that sentiment. So let's make a purposeful decision to not allow unnecessary worry to screw with our mind. If you let it, it will push away your hero and welcome the villain. This would prevent the exact thing we would like to have happen every day: something awesome.

Stop and Smell the Roses

I know this is a popular saying, but I would suggest that there is a lot more to it than first meets the eye. Being a business coach, I interact with literally thousands of business people. Many of them are, in my opinion, on a destructive path for themselves, their families, and those around them. It's my observation that they are always on, never off: they vacation with their cell phones, take business calls while out with friends, and skip family functions due to business. I try my best to explain to them that you cannot, and should not, live this way.

My company has this reputation: we are not a workaholic

company. We certainly require our clients to work on work days, but we also require them to be off on off days. I wouldn't say that I'm an expert in everything we teach; however, this is a personal strength of mine. Part of our curriculum is eight weeks of annual vacation; I have no desire for our clients, or for me, to work all the time. It's not healthy for you or your business.

On work days we expect perseverance from our clients, and you should have that expectation of yourself. However, personal days are different. They are your mental exhale days. They are your time to relax and smell the roses, whether you are fishing, gardening, playing with the kids, reading, spending time with your significant other, or playing a round of golf. For your overall personal and business health, this is required a lot more often than you might think.

When they first hear this type of message, a lot of people tell me they look forward to being in the position to follow this subscribed path of "work hard play hard" in the future. I understand—I really do. Albeit incorrect, they think the point is to work really hard for a period of time, perhaps 3–5 years, and then be in a position to take more time off: welcome to 1980's thinking.

The truth is, if you would like to achieve your goals sooner, you should implement this philosophy of stopping to smell the roses. Your brain requires down time. It does not want to be permanently on: it wants to work hard on work days and recharge on fun days. It prefers 100% on and then 100% off, which is optimal. Fortunately for you, it's also fun and fulfilling.

When your mind is clear, focussed, and refreshed you are much more likely to notice awesome things in your daily path. It makes me wonder how many awesome things go unnoticed by the person who has stacked too many days in a row of hard work and focus and has not recently stopped to smell the roses.

It's been said that you should count your blessings every day; I personally think that's a really good idea. However, it might be challenging to count your blessings if you are not even taking the time to stop and acknowledge them.

This chapter is about *your life's journey*, and that journey includes both business and personal accomplishments; it's not just about business. When you are old and reflect on a life well-lived, it's the personal accomplishments you will cherish, not the business ones!

Today is What You Have

This book is about living every day with the absolute expectation that something awesome is going to happen today. It really is about your mindset and what you are on the lookout for. Are you agonizing over something negative that has entered your life, such as a recent mental hurt from someone close to you? We cannot stop these things from happening; however, we can control how we process such challenges.

The truth is, we really just have today. Yesterday is gone: nothing can be done to alter history. We are also not guaranteed tomorrow, even if it is likely that tomorrow will be there to greet you and all your exciting future plans. Even though our future days are still likely to occur, we cannot operate in them yet. We can only move and experience what we have right now.

Of course, I have many plans for myself in all the aspects of my life, whether they are spiritual, familial, health, or business goals. I'm not saying you should ignore the future: actually, quite the opposite. Make many plans and give yourself worthwhile goals that you can work toward. Your being enjoys that. In fact, it might even be irresponsible to not set goals.

I am a personal believer in the power of future planning, and of setting goals in all the aspects of your life. However, I am also acutely aware of the fact that as exciting as those dreams may be, what I really have is today.

It would be a tragedy if people missed out on the awesome things happening today due to their regret of something in the past or from excessive focussing on the future. I have met individuals that firmly believe that their life will only be worthwhile if their perfect future comes to pass. Somehow, someway, these people feel that that their "right now" is not cutting it.

If this is you, I would recommend that you stop and write down as many items as you can about all the things you are proud of and all the good things in your life. Once you make this list, ponder it for 10 minutes. At that point, you'll realize that your current situation is actually pretty amazing.

Focussing on the future "you" is a good thing: it is the drive to improve, and the awareness that you are on this Earth to be productive and be your very best. What's not okay is thinking that the accomplishment of your dreams will somehow make your life worthwhile. Your goals are to be centered around self-improvement, not on somehow giving your life value; you already have value and purpose.

There is no doubt that awesome things cross your path on a daily basis. If they are large, you couldn't miss them if you tried: your boss calling you into their office to promote you with a substantial raise; your child being honoured for an outstanding achievement; a large business contract you have been vying for calls to inform you that you are their choice.

Regardless of your state of mind, I don't think you would miss an awesome item of this magnitude. However, on most days your awesome treat comes in a much more subtle package. If your mind is reliving a disappointment from the past, or you are living in the future, you would probably miss the little treat you could be living today.

As an example, the other day I was scheduled to teach a couple of seminars: one in the morning, and the other in the afternoon. Then I was off to the Ministry of Transportation to update my driver's license. On this particular day, a storm was brewing, with a lot of rain forecasted. Seeing as I present in a suit, I brought an umbrella that I hoped would do the job.

As I travelled to my first seminar, the skies looked ominous. I arrived: no rain yet. My umbrella remained unopened by my side. Ten minutes later, the skies opened up, and wow did it rain.

As I travelled from seminar one to talk number two, I enjoyed beautiful sunny skies. I thought to myself, "That is awesome. Massive rain, and I never experienced a drop."

When I arrived at the Ministry of Transportation, I was shocked to find that I was the only one there. When I walked in, five available tellers looked up at me. For the first time in my life I was at the Ministry and I didn't have to wait in a long line-up.

I asked the teller, "Is this normal? Because if it is, I will come at this time from now on." She responded, "Not at all; just before you arrived we were commenting on how rare this is." By the time I was done, at least 20 people were in the line-up.

When I arrived home, my wife inquired about how my day was. Because of my state of mind, I knew it had been absolutely amazing: I had avoided the rain, and for the first time in my life I had arrived at the Ministry of Transportation and was immediately the next one up. Isn't that awesome?

For you, maybe you check your garden and a few beans are ready: there's nothing better than eating something fresh that you grew. That's awesome. My point is, your daily awesome surprise will occasionally be of the bigger, more important variety. However, most days that's not the case, so you'd better be on the lookout for it. Because you can be certain that awesome things happen daily.

In a Nutshell

It would be a redundant question to ask if you would like awesome things to happen every day. But the truth is, it's our responsibility to ensure that we are in the proper frame of mind to receive our awesome daily blessing.

It's important that we don't allocate too much time to the past or to the future. Today must be given its due, so the onus is on us to make sure that every day we stop and smell the roses.

It's our job to purposefully be on the lookout for awesome things. We certainly won't miss life's big rewards, but most of our awesome things actually come in much smaller packages. It's amazing how much personal satisfaction we can receive from smaller victories.

Yesterday is gone. Tomorrow is not guaranteed. Today is what you have, and so you need to take advantage of it. Today possesses something awesome for you: I suggest you find it.

Helpful Exercise

Decide on 3 things that you would like to have in your life. They can be in any of the multiple aspects that make up your overall well-being. Itemize some rewards for yourself along the way.

Desired Item #1: _____
Finish Date: _____
Rewards Along the Way: _____
_____
_____

Desired Item #2: _____
Finish Date: _____
Rewards Along the Way: _____
_____
_____

Desired Item #3: _____
Finish Date: _____
Rewards Along the Way: _____
_____
_____

If it's not going to be fun, what's the point?

If we had it all figured out today, what would be the point of tomorrow? Enjoy the process of being a work in progress.

Unknown

Chapter Two

EVERYBODY QUALIFIES

IT'S INTERESTING FOR me to hear people try to rationalize how they are somehow exempt from life's daily awesome visitors. They say things like, "This is good enough for me," or "I could never have that." This book is about *Expecting Awesome Daily*, be it from the large, but infrequent, events or the small, but still gratifying, occurrences that are more common.

When we have the "this is good enough for me" mindset, we potentially block out life's major accomplishments as well as those daily enjoyable situations. It would be unfortunate for someone to miss out on life's daily benefits due to a misguided belief that they somehow don't qualify to receive them.

Everybody qualifies to have something awesome happen to them daily: everyone is in the game. Of course, there are many different stations in life, whether we are talking about your employment, social standing, or financial situation. Maybe you're the richest person you know, or perhaps your vocation is a little more modest. Maybe you're retired and just making ends meet. This book is a guide to *Expecting Awesome Daily*, not one to collecting riches: it's my thoughts on living every day with the absolute expectation that something awesome is going to happen.

The other day, I was in a hurry to get home after teaching a few seminars. At both seminars, many participants signed up for our program, which was awesome. However, I made the mistake of travelling too fast and was pulled over.

In my heart, I knew immediately that I was in the wrong: this was on me. I had definitely been travelling too fast, since my mind was in such a hurry. And so I was very surprised when I was let off with only a warning. The officer looked at me strangely when I said, "You are my awesome thing today."

When I arrived home, my wife inquired about my day. My response was, "It's raining awesome today." Even if the officer had given me the ticket I deserved, my response would have been the same: it's raining awesome today.

Don't get me wrong: I did appreciate the warning instead of the ticket. However, if I had not been given the pass it would not have changed my mind. My response to my wife would just have been slightly different: "It's raining awesome—oh, and I got a ticket."

I just want to be clear that those who can play the *Expecting Awesome Daily* game are not a select group: *everybody qualifies*. This includes you. Which means that today you have a choice: to either purposefully be on the lookout for something awesome, or to take the opposite route and be cynical about everything and everyone. You probably know this person: a friend or family member maybe. It's the person you do your best to avoid. I would recommend you be the person on the search daily for awesome things; the cynical group is already over-filled.

What You Deserve

Seeing as you were born on Planet Earth, there are some rights that come along with that. One of them is to have awesome things occur on a daily basis. I'm always very careful to explain my belief that everybody deserves the ability to enjoy life's daily pleasures: and no one deserves it more than you. Enjoyment in life is available to everyone.

It's a fine line between realizing that you deserve to have as much happiness as the next person and being entitled. I'm all for the "life's for everyone to enjoy" perspective; I'm against the entitlement mindset.

If you are having a hard time deciphering the difference between the two, let me help you. A person on a quest to enjoy life's daily experiences will be in motion. They will be moving both mentally and physically toward favourable experiences. On the other hand, an entitled mind tends to wait, expecting everything to come to them. They believe that awesome encounters are required to seek them out.

What I'm saying is that you deserve awesome experiences, but to do so you must be in motion. Everything in nature that is still becomes stagnant; everything that is in motion becomes vibrant. In the wild, animals must search for food or they die. For this reason, entitlement has not caught on beyond humans.

If you are not in the habit of being a person in motion—if you have somehow made the mistake of slipping into the entitlement mindset—then you will be pleasantly surprised by how many awesome surprises await you daily when you transition on purpose to being an individual in motion. Most people then realize that the awesome events were always there; they were just hidden in the cloud of inactivity.

Don't Be a Smaller Version of Yourself

When you are purposefully on the lookout for daily awesome encounters, you are in a mental state of optimal performance: every fibre of your being is in action mode. You are operating in a state of expectation, proactively on the lookout for an awesome event. Over time, operating in this high-octane mindset will illuminate the awesome opportunities that were already present.

On the other hand, if you choose a passive wait-and-see attitude, if you make awesome experiences find you and smack you in the side of the head instead of proactively looking for them, I think you would agree that a lot fewer awesome events would be discovered.

The end result is you would become a smaller version of yourself. I don't really mean having less money, fewer friends, or less opportunity (although that would probably be true). I'm talking about an overall smaller version of yourself in every aspect of your life.

This smaller version of you would still be you, and it may even be quite good. Perhaps you are physically in decent shape, financially well off, and socially possess working relationships: life's good. The problem with those that settle for the smaller version of themselves is that, in their heart, they really would prefer to be a bigger player. Perhaps their true desire is to help others, either financially or with their time; unfortunately, the smaller version of themselves doesn't possess the time or resources.

Don't get me wrong: I realize that most people living out the smaller versions of themselves are good people with good families making a positive impact on those around them. However, they know that they really had much bigger plans.

Those who deliberately seek awesome events daily are those who maximize life: they are the ones who rise above mediocrity and excel. They are the group that not only supplies for themselves, but also affect others in a positive way.

On the other hand, those who have a "just make it through the day" attitude will never experience life at its best. I'm not saying life won't be good: I'm just saying it won't be at its maximum capacity.

You do have a choice: you can either experience life at its maximum capacity or take it in on a smaller scale, resulting in a much smaller version of yourself. I would recommend that you choose to experience life at its greatest on every level. Take out your metaphorical umbrella every day, because it's raining awesome.

You Have a Choice

Throughout all of my books, the idea that you have a choice is a common theme. At the end of the day, it's up to you to spin things a certain way in your brain. You can spin things positively or, just as easily, see everything from a negative viewpoint.

Life is much more fulfilling when you are purposefully on the hunt for awesome daily occurrences instead of becoming tangled up in the "what can go wrong, will go wrong" kind of thinking. The funny thing is that even positive, motivated people accidently spin things wrong all the time: everybody does it.

It's important that we consciously make the decision to view our daily encounters in a positive fashion. I realize the vast majority of people do not live their lives to this standard, but that's why we read books.

To be clear, the ball is squarely in your court. You are 100% in control of your thinking, be it positive or negative. Most situations operate outside of your authority, but not your thinking: that is within your realm of control.

Every day you have the choice to either put on your metaphorical hunting gear and go after awesome events, or spend yet another day hunkered down in your comfort zone. I realize that the comfort zone is comfortable: that's why they call it that. Unfortunately, nothing grows there.

People who spend all their days occupying their comfort zone are the ones who have made a conscious decision to accept a smaller version of themselves. I do not recommend you join that club.

Don't Hinder Your Positive Impact

By not understanding that *everybody qualifies* for daily awesome events, and thus choosing to look for yours, you hinder your positive impact on those around you. Everyone would love to be seen as a leader: someone who others look to when guidance or direction is needed. While you read this book, you should be thinking, "Yes I would like to be that person—the one that others go to in times of physical or mental turmoil."

If you can accept and apply the principles covered in this book, if you can make some minor adjustments and purposefully be the person who realizes that they qualify as a leader, then (like all leaders) you will have honed the skill of always looking for the positive. In doing so, you will be actively on the lookout for awesome things on a daily basis. When you conduct yourself in this manner, others will automatically be drawn to you in times of trouble. Being a leader isn't something you announce or apply for: it's something that others see in you.

If you don't make a conscious decision to be a leader, to experience that metaphorical downpour of awesome events and always look on a positive point of view, others will not see your leadership capabilities. And for good reason: they would not be on display.

By simply not making that daily, conscious decision to operate your life on the positive side of the ledger, you could go your entire life and never experience the fulfillment of assisting others through a life challenge. You would, in fact, hinder the positive impact your heart truly desires.

Unfortunately, I feel like I am speaking to most people here: I think most get caught in the daily grind and never rise above it. But *everybody qualifies*. It's a daily decision, and I would recommend that you make it: you were built for this.

In a Nutshell

In our quest to create the mindset that awesome things happen every day (and that we must deliberately pursue them), we have to realize that we are in no way exempt; *everybody qualifies*. You don't have to prove yourself in any way, because you deserve as much joy and fulfillment as the next person. You simply need to step up to the plate and make a conscious decision every morning: a decision to look for the awesome in everything, and to be grateful that it's raining awesome.

Helpful Exercise

It's common for all of us to accidently sell ourselves short in certain areas of our lives. This chapter is designed to shine a light on some of those areas and correct them. Itemize 3 places where you have inadvertently sold yourself short, and the steps you will actively take to remedy your error.

Item #1 to Be Fixed: _____
Solution: _____
_____
_____

Item #2 to Be Fixed: _____
Solution: _____
_____
_____

Item #3 to Be Fixed: _____
Solution: _____
_____
_____

Selling yourself short is not the problem: staying there is!

Never settle for being a character in someone else's story when you are meant to be the author of your own.

Unknown

Chapter Three

NOW IS THE TIME

IN OUR QUEST to experience awesome adventures every day, we need to escape from the "someday" line of thinking. It's amazing to me how often I hear folks tell me about what they *intend* to do. My question is, "When?" This is commonly followed by a short pause as they realize they haven't set a timeline.

I know everyone would love to experience excitement on a regular basis: to actually *Expect Awesome Daily*. One of the most common obstacles is the "someday" mindset. Instead we need to be thinking *now is the time*.

Everyone has plans for their life. Therefore, we would do well to grasp onto the *now is the time* line of thinking and dispense of the "someday" trap. Obviously, many items will still occupy the future: even I possess a detailed list of things to do, places to go, and items to own that will unfold over the next couple of years and beyond. What I'm saying is it's a danger when *everything* occupies the future. Many of life's pleasures are for now; not all hold a future date.

The person you are committed to becoming can be the person you are today. It's true that a host of your life's experiences will unfold on a future date; however, the "you" that you are trying to create already exists. The only thing you are short on is some experiences.

My concern for people is that they live their entire lives thinking about what could happen "someday" and not enough about what is happening right now; they don't have enough focus on today.

Living your life in the future, constantly dreaming of what could be, is like traveling in your car to an exciting destination and never being able to arrive.

For many of your aspirations, my question is: what are you waiting for? What has to happen for you to take some action today?

The other day, I was teaching a seminar at an office I had not been to for several months. In my previous meeting, a salesman had asked for some guidance, to which I gladly gave them some direction. That same salesman asked the same question several months later at this seminar. In my discussion with him after the fact, I asked if he had been at all uncertain the last time we had discussed the solution to his challenge.

Unfortunately, the solution was very clear to him. It would have been better if it were unclear—or at least, uncertain of which way to go. But sadly he did have the solution; he just had not implemented it. This, in turn, meant that he had carried the unnecessary problem with him for several additional months.

This example is exactly what I'm talking about: any item that is not scheduled to occur at a specific date in the future should be solved today. *Now is the time*. I would have greatly preferred to have had a conversation with this salesman about personal advancement and how solving that challenge had launched him in a new direction. Instead, a few months had passed and nothing had progressed. Even though the solution had been clearly understood and easily applied, it was placed in the future rather than the now.

Everyone talks about what they *will* do, so our goal is to transition to being a doer, not just a talker. Even if many goals reside in the future, the date for many actions is today.

Many factors play into why some people procrastinate, be it their personality style or behaviour characteristics. However, you must understand that although certain personalities or traits might make you more susceptible to procrastination, it's not an absolute. Whether you are susceptible or not, you can still make a decision to not procrastinate. You can make the decision to deal with today's items today, so that they don't join the items that are already scheduled for future days.

No Regrets

It's been said that we regret what we have not done in life rather than what we did do. Although this is not a green light to do as you please, there is a lesson to be learned here.

When I was in my early twenties, my wife and I contributed our time to the church we attended. Specifically, we assisted church-going youths with spiritual guidance and overall direction. One of our annual activities was to visit a local senior's home around the Christmas season. The residents loved it. Truth be told, I don't think we were very good, but they didn't care; they were just appreciative of the time that we took to entertain them.

I couldn't help but notice how often the elderly folks commented to us that we needed to do things while we are young. I could plainly see that they had some regrets about not taking advantage of the opportunities they'd had in their younger years; it was clearly important to them that they impart this wisdom on to us so that we didn't make the same mistakes.

It was a number of years later that I realized the scope of the impact these experiences had on my personal outlook of doing things now. It is important not to put things off: don't be the person engaged in the dream-stealing activity of procrastination.

It's interesting that in these conversations with dozens of elderly folks, not even one shared a story of something they had done that they'd come to regret. Of course, they must have had some—everybody does—but it's interesting that, later in life, it's the things that we didn't do that we grow to regret: not the things we did.

I'm not saying that some people haven't done things that, on some level, they regret; that would be impossible. I'm just saying that, of the run-of-the-mill activities, it's what you don't do when you have the opportunity to that you will regret in your golden years.

If we sincerely want to be a person who *Expects Awesome Daily*, we must get into the habit of being a doer. Yes, thinking and planning are required, but at some point action is required too. Do it now: do what you can so that your most common retirement activity is not regret. *Now is the time*!

If It's Not in My Schedule, It Doesn't Exist

Sometimes, you hear someone say something and it changes everything for you. Sometimes, it's a new thought that takes your mind in a whole new direction. Sometimes, it's a statement that confirms how you feel and solidifies your stance on a particular opinion.

The latter is the case for me. I have always believed that it's important to have a schedule: to have your plans on paper, whether that's on a daily basis or a larger scale.

A number of years ago, I attended a large sales seminar. An amazing, powerful woman from Chicago, Anne, was on stage. She told us all, quite frankly: "If it's not in your schedule, it doesn't exist."

This stunned the crowd. Given that it was a sales seminar, participants like me understood the importance of having a schedule: in fact, we all knew that a schedule was actually very important. The stunning part was the level that Anne took it: "If it's not in your schedule, it doesn't exist." That was the level that we, as believers of writing things down and being organized, needed to take it. "If it's not in your schedule, it doesn't exist."

That statement has become a bit of a mantra with that particular company. As some participants have moved on, many starting their own companies (myself included), we have brought that truth with us.

Obviously everyone would like to have awesome things happen to them daily: that's a given. We have so many plans and ideas. And we must write them down. We must put them to paper and create a path. If it's not in my schedule, it doesn't exist. Thanks, Anne.

Let Yourself Off the Leash

We could do ourselves a big favour if we would just let ourselves off the leash every now and again. There are people who seem to be genetically wired to put themselves out there on a daily basis. They don't appear to be saddled with the constant "what ifs" that plague so many of us, myself included. On a daily basis, they seem to operate void of the concern of how others will perceive them. They are free to conduct themselves without the "what ifs."

My observation of these folks is that they are somewhat unstoppable. Their days are not filled with thinking about what could go wrong. Instead, they identify (with pinpoint accuracy) what could be. I would love to say that I am one of these fortunate people. However, that would not be true; for me, it's a learned process.

Only a small percentage of the population is blessed with this strength. Over the years, my company has trained thousands of salespeople in the art of success. We have encountered several of these fortunate folks; however, this group is quite small.

The vast majority, myself included, are required to acquire this skill. We need to purposefully let ourselves off the leash every now and again, and run with those fortunate folks who don't even own a leash. Unsurprisingly, these people are constantly on the stage with me. They are the ones everyone strives to be like; they are the ones experiencing awesome daily events.

If you own a dog, then you know what I mean. There isn't a dog on the planet that doesn't enjoy a nice walk and the opportunity to mark their territory in 47 different spots. But as much as a dog enjoys a nice walk, it's obvious how much more they enjoy the chance to get off the leash: to run free and unencumbered.

I hope you don't spend your life on just a nice walk. Do yourself a favour: let yourself off the leash every once in a while or, even better, permanently.

If you wonder which group applies to you—the group that is currently running free or the group that needs to make the switch—trust me: if you were running free, you would know it.

Don't worry, I've been there; it's a learned process.

Step one: let yourself off the leash every now and again. To a certain extent, throw caution to the wind.

Positive Acts of Contribution

In a jigsaw puzzle, there are many pieces for us to connect in order to complete the big picture. The success puzzle is the same: many pieces fitting perfectly together to create the greater scenario. Random positive acts of contribution, made with purpose on any level, are an important piece of the overall bigger puzzle.

One of the things I enjoy doing is to buy random people their morning coffee. Close to my office there is a really nice café, Jolie's. John, the lawyer across the hall, and I regularly have our first cup of coffee while sitting at the counter beside the cash register and talking about sports and politics.

As people enter, seeking their first cup of the day, we inform them that their coffee's on us. If it's their first time, they ask "Why?" or "Are you sure?" but in the end we receive a sincere, "Thank you, that's awesome." I think a few regulars try to time it in the morning: it's a sure bet that if John and Rob are enjoying the day's first cup, coffee's on them.

It's funny to watch the reactions of people who do not quite know how to receive it. "Thanks, but that's okay," they'll say. At that point, Sandra, the owner, informs them that it's really not optional. With a smile, they accept.

I realize we are not changing the world with our small gesture; however, it's important to me that I'm involved in constant acts of contribution. It's critical that I get my head in a contribution mindset as early as possible on a daily basis.

It's interesting that those patrons receiving an unexpected free coffee always use the word "awesome" in their thank you: "Wow that's awesome, thank you." Although they're the ones receiving the tangible benefit of coffee, in the bigger picture of the success puzzle it's the giver who benefits on a higher level from this small, somewhat insignificant act of contribution.

Life will, of course, afford some larger opportunities for you to be involved in acts of positive contribution. If they are already a normal way of life for you, you will be much more likely to make the correct decision and donate some of your resources, be it money, time, knowledge, or possessions.

Expecting Awesome Daily is as much about what we give out as what we receive. I don't have to ask you if you would like to have something awesome visit you on a daily basis: that would be a crazy, rhetorical question. Understand that there are many pieces in the success puzzle that make it so: contribution is one of them. The size of the contribution is not the point: possessing the heart of a contributor is.

You can start this process at any time. I'd suggest you not waste one more day: make your first random act of contribution today, on purpose, and set the wheels in motion.

Having Things Will Not Make You Happy

I should first clarify that having things is not a problem; I'm just saying that the collection of things is not where fulfillment resides. Some of the grumpiest people I know are those who seemingly gave it all, yet still don't appear to be happy.

We can learn a lot from nature in this way. Take the Dead Sea, for example. It is exactly that: dead. The Sea of Galilee is quite the opposite: flourishing with life. The interesting thing here is that both bodies of water are fed by the headwaters of the Jordan River. If the same water flows in, then why is one stagnant and dead while the other vibrant and alive? One of the primary reasons, among others, is that the Dead Sea does not have an outlet: it doesn't give, it just receives.

On the other hand, the Sea of Galilee has an outlet: it receives, it gives, and it lives vibrantly. There is a lesson for us here: we can't just hoard what we receive and expect to live that exciting life full of daily awesome experiences.

Again, I have no problem with the possessing of many items and a quality financial position. What I'm talking about is a hoarding mindset. As I like to say, "You never see a hearse pulling a U-Haul." You can't take it with you.

I'm equally not saying that you should give all your resources away: there is a balance to be had here. We can have our cake and eat it, too. You can work hard at building a high quality of life for you and your family, full of all the comforts and security you need. But all the while, you must adhere to the principle of being a person of contribution. There will be many days where the awesome thing you experience won't be something that you receive—it will be something that you do.

Make a decision today: be the Sea of Galilee, not the Dead Sea!

Each Day is a Small Step

One of my favourite sayings is, "You don't have to go from zero to hero." All we really have to do is move in the correct direction. People are often too impatient with themselves, others, and their personal circumstances. We need to make a connection to the power behind the process. It's important to enjoy the journey: far too many people seem to only be satisfied when an endeavour has been accomplished.

There are multiple problems with this approach. First off, a sense of anxiousness will be prevalent throughout your journey until you meet your goal. Secondly, you will simply not have enough senses of accomplishment.

In our quest for success, it's important to celebrate the small victories along the way. Those times of celebration can come in small, physical rewards or mental acknowledgment, but either way it's a lot more fun to enjoy these small advances than not.

As an example, if a person's desire was to pay off their mortgage, it would be wise to set a plan with small steps and rewards on a regular basis. That way, you will enjoy a small sense of accomplishment each time a smaller portion is contributed to the overall goal instead of only one big moment of gratification when you make your final instalment on some date probably quite a bit in the future.

This book is about *Expecting Awesome Daily*, so it's important that you deliberately construct your life to play out accordingly. If your goal is to pay off that mortgage, and your plan is to put aside $2,000 per month with another 10 years left in your loan, that would be 120 instalments of $2,000. Much better to feel great about 120 accomplishments, each a little less than the final overall goal, than just the one feeling of success after 10 years at the end.

There is no doubt that the brain that *Expects Awesome Daily* thinks in a certain way. That, in and of itself, is a step in the right direction, because it in turn activates the law of attraction to help you bring about the desired awesome daily events.

However, it's also true that you can, and should, set up your life with these small steps of accomplishment to be a part of your daily awesomeness. In the previous illustration, the accomplishment of eliminating that mortgage would have 120 spaced out awesome achievements and one large one at the end: that's 120 awesome daily events that are already accounted for, and thus you are not required to attract.

What if all your goals in every aspect of your life possessed this kind of structure? If each of them allowed for many smaller senses of accomplishment along the way, all culminating in a larger sense of satisfaction when the itemized goal is realized? Those are far more instances of daily awesome than if you just had one big accomplishment at the end of each.

It's true that the law of attraction will still do its job if you are thinking correctly. However, it would also be wise to augment life's attracted awesome moments with those we have already set in place.

This is the reason that I can say that the journey is as much fun as the destination. The celebrating of the smaller steps along the way allows you to enjoy every part of the accomplishment, not just the final result.

Think about how much your mind plays into *Expecting Awesome Daily*. Then think about all those worthwhile goals in the multiple aspects of your life, all broken up into smaller, achievable pieces. Each smaller portion adds upon the other. That's a lot of positivity to add to your mindset. With that structure, you are doing your brain a big favour by not withholding all sense of accomplishment until the entire goal has been met.

It's important that your structure is specific and actionable. For example, if your goal is to pay off that mortgage, it's wise to say "I will make a $2,000 payment on the 15th of each month," as opposed to "I will put money toward that goal whenever I have some extra on hand."

Think about all the aspects of your life this way, be it finances, physical condition, spiritual position, family, or relationships. If each aspect has a plan with milestone stops along the way, that's a lot of awesome purposefully built into your life.

You can have it all: you just can't have it all today. And you shouldn't need it all in order to be satisfied. Your satisfaction should come in the form of small accomplishments along the way as each step is checked off the list. Enjoy the small steps each day!

In a Nutshell

In our quest to *Expect Awesome Daily*, we must grasp the reality that *now is the time*. It's important that we don't fall into the all-too-popular trap of putting things off into the future. Your future contains a whole bunch of things that will require your attention and time. We must accept the reality that those items on today's agenda must be dealt with today. *Now is the time.*

In our journey of *Expecting Awesome Daily*, we must complete tasks in an appropriate timeframe: procrastination is the chief killer of dreams. *Now is the time* for awesome daily awareness: leave no regrets as you move forward and accomplish each day's small, allocated steps.

Let yourself off the leash, get your mind going, and be a person of accomplishment. Don't put things off: be a doer, not a talker. *Now is the time*!

Helpful Exercise

We all make the mistake of putting off items that, in our hearts, we know should have been dealt with a long time ago. We are also acutely aware that this problem is not going to solve itself. So I want you to decide on one thing that you will commit to taking action on today.

Item I am going to take action on today: _____

What action will be taken: _____

Let's not make things complicated: simply decide on the item you are going to target today and the appropriate action.

No more wasting time: let's get it done!

The really happy people are those who have broken the chains of procrastination, those who find satisfaction in doing the job at hand. They're full of eagerness, zest, productivity. You can be, too.

Norman Vincent Peale

Chapter Four

PERSPECTIVE IS EVERYTHING

HOW WE VIEW events makes all the difference in the world. There's a cute little joke of a turtle who was mugged on the beach by a marauding band of snails. When asked what happened in the interview afterward, the turtle said, "I don't know—it all happened so fast."

From the turtle's perspective it was fast; from our point of view, it would be difficult to watch.

If we all sat in a big circle and threw our problems in the centre, once we had a chance to see everyone else's problems, we would probably grab ours back pretty fast. Without the ability to view others' circumstances, our personal challenges appear greater than they actually are. Only after we get the opportunity to view others' life obstacles are we in a position to put our personal situations in perspective.

Obviously, this is never going to happen literally. Therefore, we need a method of categorizing the severity of our challenges without the opportunity of directly comparing it to the struggles others are experiencing.

I heard another cute story that brings the concept of perspective home quite nicely. There was once a store where you were permitted to bring in the cross you are bearing and switch it for another one. The goal was to leave with a more manageable cross than the one you had.

A gentleman enters the store. "I'm here to trade my cross for another," he says.

"They're all in the back," responds the clerk. "All of them there are available."

The gentleman sets down his cross. He is quite pleased that he has finally gotten the chance to make a switch. He feels that he has exhausted all of his options with this particular cross.

As he peruses his options in the stack of available crosses, he notices a very small cross off by itself. "Perfect," he says as he picks it up. He can't help but notice how much lighter this cross is.

He makes his way to the door. Just before he exits, the clerk says, "Hey, where are you going with that cross?"

The gentleman responds, "This is the one I wish to switch for."

"You can't leave with that one," the clerk says.

Confused, the gentleman inquires as to why. "It was my understanding that all the crosses were available to me," he says.

And the clerk tells him: "Yes, they were all available to switch. But that is the cross you brought in."

I'm not making light of our challenges. I'm just saying that perspective is an interesting thing, and often our over-dramatic minds elevate issues to a higher elevation than they may deserve. Maybe the cross you bear is a large one, or maybe your cross is small and just built up in your mind to appear as if it were a large one.

Even if it is a small cross, it's still a cross you are bearing. I'm not suggesting the cross is imaginary—I'm just pointing out that with a different perspective, it might become a lot more manageable.

In our quest for *Expecting Awesome Daily*, a common stumbling block will be the tendency to build up events and circumstances to be larger than they deserve.

Success Comes in Cans

When my children were younger, they competed in competitive trampoline. Whenever their coach showed them new tricks and techniques, they often said, "I can't do that."

I loved the coach's response: "Success comes in 'cans,' not 'can'ts.' Give me 20 push ups." It didn't take the students long to eliminate "I can't" from their vocabulary.

Instead, we should add the word "yet" to the end of any sentence we say about something that currently resides outside of our skill set. "I can't ride a bike without my training wheels" versus "I can't ride a bike without my training wheels yet." Or "I don't understand this math" versus "I don't understand this math yet."

Adding "yet" to the end of any statement changes everything. Without "yet," you are accepting defeat; but by adding the word "yet," you are informing the challenge that you are coming for it: its days are numbered.

Glass Half-Full

"Be a glass half-full instead of a glass half-empty" is a commonly-used saying; we all know what it means. If I were to ask 100 people if they are a glass-half-full or a glass-half-empty person, all 100 would say "Half-full, of course."

Unfortunately, they would not all be correct: the truth is, the vast majority of people are half-empty dwellers. However, saying that you are a glass-half-empty person isn't the kind of thing that you want to admit.

Conditioning plays a big part in the mindset of human beings. For instance, the evening news is nothing more than a collection of catastrophes currently taking place. Of course, there is no shortage of positive, uplifting events also occurring. But good news isn't news.

Even something as simple as the weather report is spun in the glass-half-empty format: Saturday has a 10% chance of rain. People will cancel their outdoor activities, when in fact there is a 90% chance it's not going to rain!

As we interact with others on a daily basis, we are subjected to glass-half-empty people regularly. So often, in fact, that the half-full people can sometimes be hard to find. Over time, the constant barrage of negative people and information can take its toll, and before you know it, you have joined the glass-half-empty club. I go as far as to say the glass half-empty is a predictable destination.

We must make a conscious decision to become a member of the glass-half-full fraternity; trust me, there's lots of room. I can't understate the importance of purposefully taking the path less travelled in this regard: go in the opposite direction of the masses.

No one gets to live forever. All of our time is limited, so it's important that we do it correctly. I know you would love to have awesome events happen to you every day. I know you would also agree that living in a constant state of glass half-empty would effectively camouflage all the everyday goodness there is and allow it to slip by undetected.

Instead, make the conscious decision to run with those who see opportunity where others see obstacles. It illuminates the awesome daily occurrences as opposed to hiding them.

So take the path less travelled: fight the daily urge to melt into the masses and conform to accepting the fate of the glass-half-empty people. Be different. Be a leader.

King of the Jungle

Everyone knows the lion holds this title. As the undisputed king of the jungle, the lion possesses the luxury of not having to look over his shoulder; nothing is coming for the lion.

It's common on nature shows to see the lion sprawled out under a tree, enjoying the shade or fast asleep. They've not a care about their safety. It's important to understand that the lion is not the biggest animal on the grasslands, or even the strongest: yet he is the undisputed king.

What the lion has is attitude, and lots of it. We could learn a lot from the lion. We don't have to be the smartest, best-looking, or even the most talented: what we do need is an attitude, and a good one at that!

If our goal is to be on the lookout for awesome events on a daily basis, it's imperative that our attitude is conducive to obtaining this desired outcome. I can't say for certain what goes on in a lion's mind, but I'm pretty sure they're quite aware that they are in charge.

I'm not saying that we should have an "I'm better than everyone else" attitude. In fact, I'm not saying that. What I am saying is our attitude should be strong and powerful, even though we know we are not the strongest, best-looking, or even the most talented.

The lion's perspective is "I am in charge." We should think that way—be the king of the jungle.

You Have a Choice

This particular thought, you have a choice, is so important that it weaves through all my books, materials, and talks I deliver, and bears repeating here. At the end of the day, it's up to you. Ultimately, you have a choice: you can *Expect Awesome Daily* or you can be on the lookout for situations to go wrong and work against you; it's your choice.

When I get the opportunity to speak with those who have the luxury to live well into their nineties or better, they all seem to be so positive and have so much wisdom to offer. It's almost as if the negative-minded group have long since passed. I don't have any medical background, so my knowledge in this area is beyond limited, but I can't help but notice that those who live vibrant lives well past their peers reside in the glass-half-full group.

We have a choice in our perspective and which way we want to spin events.

This isn't something we can change overnight; nor do we need to. We just need to make a conscious decision to view circumstances from a healthy point of view. So look on the bright side, and be a glass-half-full person. And be forgiving with yourself. If you are a positive person overall, don't fall into the trap of the "woe is me" attitude just because you've made one mistake. This is the end result of the glass-half-empty thinker. Be patient: it's not important that you make the change today, it's just important that you make the change.

So don't sell yourself short. The choice is clearly yours, and you do possess the power to make the necessary switch.

Scarecrow

In my first book, *The Grass is Greener on This Side of the Fence*, "A Scarecrow Never Harmed a Crow" is one of the chapters. The point I make is that although in the mind of the crow scarecrows are very real and very scary, we, of course, know that it doesn't pose any danger to the crow. The scarecrow is nothing more than a few sticks, a hat, shirt, and some straw.

The fact that we know this is no help to the crow, however: to them, it's very real. From their perspective, they are in mortal danger.

Scarecrows aren't effective because they're real; it's because from the perspective of the crow they're real. That's all that really matters to the farmer.

There's something I feel I should point out in this metaphor: scarecrows are strategically placed to be exactly where crows will find food. If the crows could sort out their perspective, all they would need to do is fly around and look for scarecrows.

This makes me wonder where in our personal lives we may have erected a scarecrow. Like the crows, maybe the place where we have manufactured a scarecrow is, in fact, the exact location where we should be heading. Just a thought! *Perspective is everything.*

Living a Life of Balance

Expecting Awesome Daily applies to all the aspects of our lives, be it business, health, family, relationships, or spiritual position. Since it affects all of these aspects, it's important that we purposefully select the positive point of view, giving us an uplifting perspective in all situations and circumstances.

I hear the word "balance" a lot in the circles I travel. It is exactly what I am referring to: living a life of balance. As I travel around to address audiences, I find it interesting to see the sheer number of people in search of the elusive feeling of balance.

I have some good news for you: balance is nothing more than a feeling of content, specifically with regard to the aspects of your life. Let's pretend that your business or employment is going okay, you are in decent shape, your family might be a bit crazy (like mine), but all right overall, and you have made peace with your spiritual position. If that's you, maybe everything isn't quite perfect; however, life is good. The mood of your quiet time will be that of contentment; in other words, balance.

In think some people perceive balance as something that occurs when everything is perfect. Well I say good luck with that!

Balance is when you have contentment—not perfection, but contentment. Balance is also a state of mind, not an amount in your bank account.

When you take a look at all the aspects of your life, how you view what has happened in those areas will go a long way to create contentment. For example, my immediate and extended family are amazing—I wouldn't change them for the world—but believe me when I tell you we have some characters. I now have a choice: will I only consider them acceptable if everyone lives their lives to my principles and standards?

If I take this perspective, I will never be content with regard to my family, since they're not all to my standard of perfection. It's worth noting, in this case, that to some of them I'm the odd one.

If your life seems to lack balance and contentment, you may

be creating some undue stress in certain aspects of your life due to an incorrect perspective. Examine the aspects of your life and your perspective. Are you in balance?

Same Situation, Different Perspective

I heard a story the other day about the different paths in life that two brothers took based on a personal situation they simultaneously experienced. The fact that they were twins, making them extra close, makes this story all the more extraordinary.

When they were young, theirs was the regular life of young boys: days spent getting dirty, getting into trouble, and participating in sports. One day, however, would prove to be too challenging: the day they found out their father was a serial killer; difficult, I'm sure, for any family to accept.

The interesting part of this story came many years later, when a psychological study proposed to find out what had become of the boys.

Child number one became a very successful businessman, and accomplished in many aspects of his life. The question was asked of him what impact he thought his father being a convicted serial killer had had on him.

The response was quite logical: how else could he have turned out? Seeing as his father was a serial killer, he had to specifically make an effort to move in the opposite direction. Personally, I think the response makes sense.

Child number two had gone down a totally different path. He himself had committed crimes, and was interviewed from jail. When asked the same question as his brother, his response was the same: since his father was a serial killer, how else could his life have turned out?

They each had their own valid point; the only difference was their perspective of the situation. It's the same event, but a different result because of their perspective.

Even though I'm using a tragic situation, the point I'm making is that they both have the same reason. Brother number one: based on the events, how else could I turn out? Brother number two: based on the events, how else could I turn out?

In our quest for *Expecting Awesome Daily*, we do have some control over our perspective; when events occur, we need to move in the positive direction instead of the negative. The perspective you accept will have far-reaching consequences.

How Things Will Be

I do get asked a lot to help in improving one's perspective. When I deliver a talk on this topic, although I do receive some kickback, no one has ever come to me and stated, "How I view things makes no difference; that will probably never happen." To some degree, everyone agrees with this concept.

I do get a lot of people inquiring about a practical step or two that they could implement to assist them in their quest of having a more positive perspective. They are looking for a trick that will serve them well as they travel through this awesome life.

There are many things you can do; however, the most impactful is to consider the long-term effect of how your brain is spinning any particular event. If, after just a minute or two of thought, you realize that your current thinking will create a path that is less than helpful (or even harmful), then change your perspective. Explore a different path, one that leads to a more desirable outcome.

As an example, the other day during one of my seminars, a young man from the audience introduced himself at the break. He said that he was new to the industry, and that he "realized that things are very difficult when you are new."

If you're taking my point about perspective to heart, you can easily see that his perspective, of things being challenging when you're new, is going to create a host of negative circumstances for him. His brain is architecting its own demise.

On the other hand, he could just as easily have said, "I'm new to the business, and very excited. Look out business, here I come." That, of course, is nothing more than the opposite perspective.

Whichever way you spin it, you are going to be correct. So better to say "Look out, here I come."

Boat Burning

The story about Cortés invading Mexico is an excellent illustration of perspective. According to stories, he landed on a beach with all of his men. The Mexicans, viewing the goings-on from a distance, would of course feel a certain amount of stress at being invaded. However, seeing as they outnumbered Cortés and his men, which is always a plus, it's probably safe to say they started out at least somewhat confident.

As the story goes, Cortés ordered the boats to be burned, eliminating their option to retreat. Cortés and his men now only had one perspective: they were going to win. As the Mexicans looked on from their (temporary) safe distance, I can't help but think that their perspective may have been altered as well—in favour of their opponent.

It's been widely proclaimed that this one move, the burning

of the boats, caused the downfall of the Mexican army and their ultimate surrender to Cortés.

I'm not making this claim; I'm simply pointing out the adjustment in perspective that the burning of the boats must have created in the minds of the Spaniards and the Mexicans. Perhaps victory was inevitable for Cortés; however, a display of confidence like eliminating your escape route couldn't have hurt.

In our quest to *Expect Awesome Daily*, our perspective will play a large part in the equation. For instance, once the boats were lit, the Mexicans' changed perspectives likely dashed their chance of something awesome happening on that particular day.

That Seems Unfair

The truth is, sometimes things actually are unfair. Sometimes, maybe quite often, you experience a situation that has you on the wrong side, through no fault of your own. This isn't a rare occurrence; in fact, it's quite common. Life will occasionally deal you a blow, and you won't have done anything to create the situation that caused it; it will just happen. I can think of several personal stories that fit these criteria within the last month, they are that common.

Although it may be true that we have played no part in the creation of our current dilemma, we do still choose how we interpret it. We have 100% control over our perspective. So although we may or may not have played a part in architecting the situation, we are the ones who determine where we go from there.

There is a saying: "don't add fuel to the fire." I think that it applies here. If our perspective of a situation is unhealthy, in all likelihood we'll make it worse—or at least delay the healing process. I'm not saying you should not have a reaction to negative life situations. I'm just saying that the sooner we can put them in the rear view mirror, the better. The more healthy perspectives are the more expedient solutions.

Life's too short to bog ourselves down with issues that won't really matter in the long run. All we really do is cloud our brain with unnecessary feelings of anger, revenge, or spite, which, in turn, block our ability to *Expect Awesome Daily*.

It's always better to proactively look for solutions. Be the one to purposefully inhabit a healthy perspective.

Running in Water

Nothing is more fun than soaking up the sun on a hot day while frolicking in the water. I live in Canada, so this is a three-month event. Although it's satisfying to feel the warmth of the sun on your skin, it's still difficult to run in water. Whatever fun you are having, it's still challenging to get from Point A to Point B when you're up to your waist in water.

When you accidently spin something into a negative perspective, it's like you are running in water: your mobility is greatly limited.

If something unwanted presents itself to you, the objective is to move past this intruder as efficiently as possible. Your perspective will be the deciding factor in how quickly you can create space between you and this unwanted visitor.

If your perspective is healthy and positive, you will zoom right past it; on the other hand, if your perspective leans toward the unhealthy, negative viewpoint, you are now running in water, limiting your ability to put the required distance between you and it. I think the unhealthy perspective is the most natural; you have to train your brain to travel the positive path.

Most people spend their entire lives running in water. They spend way too much of their valuable time too close to unwanted scenarios. The trick is to spin your perspective in the positive direction: get out of the metaphorical water and distance yourself as quickly as possible from life's unwanted hassles.

I realize that many of these negative situations were not your fault. Quite often you were, in fact, the victim; however, life is short. So let's not get bogged down in the water and miss life's daily awesome events.

In a Nutshell

Perspective is everything: how we spin things in our minds will dictate whether we experience awesome events daily or find ourselves wanting. It's not that awesome events will occur when our perspective is correct; these awesome visitors are present daily. But they can be hidden in a vacuum of negative thoughts that spin through our minds.

We would be wise to purposefully work on our skills at viewing circumstances with a healthy perspective. Clear your mind from damaging, negative clutter. This will, in turn, illuminate the awesome events that are present daily.

Perspective is everything!

Helpful Exercise

Both those who hit their goals on a regular basis and those who continually fall short make this mistake: the error of spinning things incorrectly in their mind. The difference is that successful people correct their thinking a lot sooner. Itemize one situation that you have accidently viewed through a negative lens. Once you have decided which circumstance to fix, we simply need to apply a better perspective.

I Totally Spun This Wrong: _____

A Better Way to View It Would Be: _____
_____

Perspective is everything!

*You don't have control over your situation.
But you have a choice about how you view it.*

Chris Pine

Chapter Five

YES YOU CAN

IT'S IMPORTANT THAT we don't listen to that small, inner voice that constantly points out our limitations, especially when it tells us that we are not as good as we think. I'm not saying to never listen to that inner voice; in fact, I have an entire line of teaching about paying attention to that voice and what it's trying to communicate to you. However, when it propagates the message that you are not good enough or can't do something, it's your job to challenge that message with energy and vigour.

I love watching nature shows, specifically those that are filmed in the wilds of Africa. A very common scene is of the large cats, be it lions or cheetahs, tracking a herd of wildebeests. It's interesting how nature is set up: the big cats are really the only predators the wildebeests face—other than man.

As the cats send the herd on the run they look to separate one for the take-down. Usually, this is pretty successful. But what if the wildebeests thought this through and refused to run? What if they came to the following realization: *Okay, there are 200 of us 4 of them; they weigh about 150 pounds each, while we weigh upwards of 600; they have sharp teeth, but we have sharp horns. Maybe we should take them down instead.*

Obviously, this would never happen; nature is not set up that way. Wildebeests are genetically inclined to fear large cats, so even though running makes no sense, they do it anyway. The good news for the big cats is the wildebeests are not going to read this chapter.

To put this in a human perspective, imagine if 4 ultimate fighters picked a fight with 200 average men. The 200 regular guys are not genetically engineered to fear other humans, so even though the 4 ultimate fighters one-to-one are superior in combat, once the fight started they would be subdued quickly.

Our dog Winnie makes it clear she does not inhabit the wildebeest mindset. The other day at the lake, I let Winnie out for her evening roam around the property. It was one of those dark, moonless nights. While she sniffed around, I could hear a few deer on the ridge about 50 metres to my right.

It didn't take Winnie long to pick up their scent. Off she went with all the energy her 14lb. frame could create. Those deer were gone in no time, and back came Winnie at a trot: mission accomplished.

Every dog is a wolf in their mind. I don't think that Winnie is aware that, at 14lbs, she isn't exactly a danger to very much. But that doesn't matter to Winnie. The *yes you can* thinking in her brain had no problem with the fact that there were 3 deer at about 150 pounds apiece. In Winnie's mind, intruders had entered the property, and it was her job to rectify the situation, which she did masterfully.

A good question to ask ourselves is whether our automatic thinking leans toward Winnie—confidence beyond what we should really have—or whether it is more like the deer and the wildebeest—fleeing from an inferior opponent.

As you continue to aspire to success, you need to understand that *yes you can* accomplish things. Although we can run away, we don't need to.

I wonder what would have happened if the deer simply refused to run. Would a 14lb dog take the three of them down? Although I'm sure she would bark at them for a while, eventually she would lose interest. What if the wildebeests turned to fight the lions? Eventually the lions would be forced to move along.

The deer and wildebeests don't need to run, but they do. So the question to ask yourself is: do you run from opportunities when you shouldn't? Do you flee when something makes you nervous, or do you dig in, stand your ground, and take a *yes I can* attitude? Is your go-to emotion courage or fear? Are you more similar to Winnie—a lion—or a wildebeest—a lion's fear-filled prey?

To live in a state where your norm is *Expecting Awesome Daily*, you are going to need to stop running away. Be that person who sees opportunity and is willing to stick it out, pay the price, and make it happen.

Everything I Need I Already Possess

Having a *yes you can* attitude isn't something you need to grow into: it's something you already possess. You don't have to read endless books or attend seminars on a regular basis in order to attain a *yes I can* attitude. I'm not saying reading and personal development isn't important; of course it is. I'm just saying that you already possess what's required to have a *yes I can* mindset.

The wildebeests don't need to work out or run every day in order to handle the lion; they are already far superior in both strength and numbers. Wildebeests will never attain the realization that everything they need they already possess: but you can. You can have that mindset. Today is the day to make the jump to that awareness.

I am a firm believer that I already possess a *yes I can* attitude and everything else I need for ultimate success. However, people will periodically question me on this belief, suggesting that maybe we possess *most* of what we need instead.

I still believe that our current position is that of possessing everything we need for ultimate success, whatever success means to that individual. However, I pick my battles and agree that we "mostly" possess everything that is needed to achieve our goals. The reason I accept this lesser reality is that it accomplishes my objective either way.

Normally, this conversation takes place with a client who does not recognize that they are a lot closer to a breakthrough than they give themselves credit for. They don't require any skills that they don't currently possess: they just need to tap into that vast reservoir that is, and has always been, available to them.

While I do my best, I am not always able to fully convince them that they already possess the ingredients required for the recipe of success. However, in many cases I am able to persuade them to the halfway point. They agree that they possess some, or maybe even most, of the necessary elements to achieve their desired goal.

At this point I usually agree; not because I think they are correct, but because I know that once they believe that they possess even some of what they require, they will have already put themselves on the path of accomplishment. Even as I agree, my heart is aware that they are in possession of much more than they could possibly imagine.

When the conversation first begins, they believe themselves to be lost: that their worthwhile goals are miles away. If I am able to convince them that they possess everything they need to conquer their obstacle, that's amazing. But even if their brain only accepts that they have most of the required skills, they are at least on the correct path.

I feel like I should be clear: I firmly believe that we do, in fact, possess everything we need for ultimate success; however, even if we can only accept that we possess some of what we require, we will still be okay. It's the "I'm a million miles away" line of thinking that's not okay.

The Inner Voice

The inner voice that never stops chatting with you can be either your best friend or your worst enemy. It's the voice that either tells you "You are amazing, with so much to offer," or "You are average at best and bring little to the table."

It's been said that life is like an echo: what you send out comes back to you. This is exactly how the inner voice works: what you think today is the conversation your inner voice will have with you in the future. Your thoughts will echo back to you. If you think positive, uplifting thoughts today, your inner voice of the future will also be positive and uplifting.

If today our inner voice is being our worst enemy, we need to look back on our previous days. If we are brutally honest with ourselves, we will see that we have previously made the mistake of thinking or, even worse, saying things that are negative or maybe even destructive. No surprise, this inner voice is pushing you away from the expectation of daily awesome.

You do have a choice. Your brain loves to be trained: it would be more than happy to echo positive, uplifting thoughts to you in your near future. You just have to do your part and think positive, uplifting thoughts today; it's really that simple.

As a business coach, I hear clients talking negatively all day. It usually takes the form of "woe is me" about how unfair life is for them. While I listen, I am aware that I am only hearing the echoes of previous negative thinking. It's like a boomerang: you send it out, and it will come right back. There is no escaping this reality.

All of us would love to have our inner voice be our ally, for it to constantly speak confidently about our abilities and build us up on a daily basis. If you want that, then you need to recognize that it is, in fact, an echo you are hearing; if you don't put it out, it can't come back to you.

If we truly want to live life *Expecting Awesome Daily*, a strong, confident inner voice is necessary.

You Are Not as Trapped as You Think

As of the writing of this book, I have been training and coaching business people for over 20 years. In that time, I have had thousands of conversations with individuals who feel "trapped." I do my best to share my insights and help free them; however, when I am dealing with someone who has been sending out negative, damaging thoughts for quite some time, I am contending with a very powerful echo.

When the circus trains an elephant, they put a cord around

its leg and fix it to a stake in the ground. If the elephant pulls on it, it cuts into their leg, so the elephant stays put. Obviously, the elephant could pull the spike out of the ground if they wanted to, but they don't. After a while, the cable is removed, and the elephant stays put without it. In the elephant's mind, staying put is associated with a lack of pain.

In reality, the elephant is free to roam; but in their head they are still tied down, so there they stay. I think we are the same way: we're not as trapped as we think. And our solution is just a little bit of positive, proactive thinking away.

Sometimes, getting a person to think positively is very difficult. Usually the conversation falls back on something like, "You don't understand: here's what has happened to me; this person did this or that..." I'm sorry to say, it doesn't matter. I don't make the rules, but what you are putting out today will echo in your future.

That feeling of being trapped is a very bad place to be; if elephants only knew that they are not confined like they think they are, they would be much better off. Even if they had decided to stay, they would be there for a whole new reason, by choice instead of being trapped.

We realize that the elephants are not really tied down, since we are smarter than they. But perhaps we need to look around for our own cord that may no longer be attached.

Procrastination is a Killer

This chapter, "*Yes You Can*," has a few enemies, and one of them is the plague of procrastination. We really need to take a good, long look at procrastination and what a stumbling block it is. It's been said that procrastination is the killer of dreams—I believe this to be true!

I have observed literally hundreds of entrepreneurs procrastinate themselves right out of the business. And of course, their new line of work is only temporary due to the habit of procrastination and its inevitable cycle. Do we procrastinate due to a lack of confidence, or do we simply not possess enough information to move forward?

If you feel it is a lack of confidence, then you need to take some time and reread this chapter. You would be wise to open up your mind and accept the fact that *yes you can*, and come to terms with the knowledge that you already possess everything you need for ultimate success.

Once you process this information, you will quickly realize that the confidence you seek currently resides inside you. Unshakable confidence isn't something to be attained: it's something to be discovered.

People can search their entire lives for something that is already embedded within them. Change your mindset from one that seeks something externally to one of self-discovery, and tap into the skills that currently lie dormant, just waiting to be discovered. Your mind may have you convinced that you are not good enough, but I'm telling you that this is not true: not only are you good enough, you already possess the very thing you are searching for.

Procrastinating due to feeling that you have insufficient knowledge is another misunderstanding you also need to sort out. I observe this condition in action on an almost daily basis. Clients stuck in a rut make the decision to procrastinate due to insufficient information.

It doesn't seem to matter how much knowledge they collect: they never take the step of implementation. I am left constantly inquiring as to when they are going make the move; it's like ready, aim ... ready, aim ... ready, aim ... Are we going to pull the trigger at some point?

The truth is, it doesn't matter how much mental processing takes place: the trigger is not going to be pulled. This condition isn't about a lack of information; it's about a lifestyle. This kind of person has created a habit of inaction, which will eventually lead to the abandonment of a worthwhile goal. Sadly, the setting of a new goal will only result in the same outcome. This chapter is about *yes you can*, but procrastination leads to the opposite: no I cannot.

A few months ago, I ran into a client at an event. They shared a short-term goal with me, and in return I gave them a simple assignment to put them on the path of achieving that worthwhile goal.

A few months later, I ran into the same client and inquired after the results. But their response was, "I'm still processing the advice you gave me, and setting a plan to implement it." My expectation was that they would have set my advice in motion the same day it was given. Had they done so, they would have already attained their goal.

This situation is exactly what I'm talking about: in their mind, they needed more data. But in fact, they had what they needed; they simply needed to apply it and move forward.

This story is so common that hundreds of clients are going to think I am talking about them. If this conversation sounds like you, please accept the premise that you already have what you need and move forward. Life is short: don't procrastinate. Implement what you have. It's enough and be *Expecting Awesome Daily*.

Stop Second-Guessing Yourself

I realize that second-guessing yourself has its place. I remember the day I went parachuting, and as we cruised thousands of feet above the ground, my mind was rightly thinking, *Is this really a good idea?*

For sure there will be times when important decisions are required and your brain, for good reason, will challenge you about the direction you are about to travel. This is healthy and completely necessary.

What I'm talking about is second-guessing yourself on life's daily decisions: those ones that occupy the smaller scale. Although they matter today, they don't play a part in the greater scheme of life. These are the decisions that we need to simply make and move forward without looking back. We need to deliberately take that step and stop labouring over every little decision.

It's been said that a bad decision is better than no decision at all. I am in full agreement. Obviously, a wrong decision on its own is a bad call; however, in the proper scale of the big picture, being a quick decision-maker who doesn't look back will result in a better outcome overall.

If we continually second-guess every twist and turn in the natural flow of life, we are never going to get anywhere. This is a hidden form of procrastination. We can set goals all day long—we can even write them down—but unfortunately our indecisive nature will be squarely in our way.

Let's face it: we are not always jumping out of airplanes. So let's not treat every decision like it's a life-or-death circumstance. If you truly want to live in a constant state of *Expecting Awesome Daily*, you need to stop second-guessing yourself and avoid mental paralysis.

You Are More Prepared Than You Think

It's interesting to me how often people believe there is a huge chasm between where they are and where they desire to be. They feel that the preparation for the big jump is immense, and so they sell themselves short, believing that they are not yet ready. This inability to acknowledge their current state of preparedness creates a dangerous mindset of "someday." Unfortunately, in this scenario, "someday" never happens.

I am not saying that I don't believe in committing to learning and instruction; after all, I do own a coaching company. Obviously I believe in travelling down a path of self-improvement, and gaining knowledge from a mentor or coach is a part of that. But although advancing your position in both knowledge and experience is vital, I would like to point out that you are not starting from ground zero; your reservoir of knowledge is not empty. You do bring something to the table; in fact, you bring a lot more than you are probably giving yourself credit for.

When clients join our coaching company, they first fill out a questionnaire on where they want to be at the end of the year, as well as several years down the road. Before their first coaching call, we are clear of their plan: their perfect scenario is already laid out for us.

The coach's job is to guide them down their desired path and ultimately arrive at their destination. It's common for clients to say, "Although I have been in the business for a number of years, treat me as though I were a new entrepreneur." But what that statement really means is "I have nothing. Everything I need to achieve my desired result is yet to be obtained." And that's not helpful.

To combat this, the coach will begin the process of drawing out their current skills. Only once we identify what we bring to the table can we evaluate what skills are yet to be obtained.

This process can be challenging for the coach at times. The

coach is aware that the new client does, in fact, bring some skills to the table. They are not starting from the beginning: they are more prepared than they think.

We do get why a new client would make the statement, "Treat me as if I were a new entrepreneur." We understand that they have laid out their ultimate dreams on the questionnaire, and that those ultimate achievements seem like they're a million miles away. This is especially true when one wants to be perceived as an absolute beginner. But even if you are new to your aspiration, you still bring a substantial set of life skills to the table.

Our coaches spend a fair bit of time early on in the process to draw out of each client the experiences and skills they already possess. This allows us to figure out where on the path to success our starting point is. Most people believe that they start from zero, which, of course, creates the illusion that the finish line is so far away.

But once you take some time to examine what you bring to the process, the truth is exposed: that you are, in fact, starting a ways down the course towards the finish line. With this in focus, perhaps you'll find that the end is actually right there on the horizon—and you've only just begun. This is usually the case, because you are more prepared than you think.

Being too hard on yourself is more common than most people realize, but thinking that you start everything from the beginning is simply not true. We all have many skills and experiences, and we need to take those into consideration prior to venturing out on any quest for improvement. So although living in a state of *Expecting Awesome Daily* may seem like a pipe dream, you should accept the fact that you are more prepared than you think.

Dreams Are in Your Mind for a Reason

The things you dream about are in your mind for a reason: if you take a good, long look at what you're trying to accomplish, 9 times out of 10 you will find that the accomplishment of said goal has substantial benefit for the others around you as well. Worthwhile goals are rarely just for you.

I'm not saying that you can't set personal goals where you're the only beneficiary; for instance, your weight or physical condition often fall into this category. But ignoring those, you'll see that many of your goals would benefit other people—or at least, they should.

Your personal income, as an example, dictates the quality of life your family experiences. Perhaps you have a goal to be an above-average provider for your immediate and extended family—a noble goal. If that is in your head, it's there for a reason. Don't just dream about it: get moving toward it. You are a lot closer than you think.

We all have ambition; it's part of being human. We also all have the opportunity to make those worthwhile goals a reality; it's really up to us.

Those goals are there for a reason. Something within you has created a scenario that, when achieved, will allow multiple people to reap the rewards. The ball is in your court: take stock of the skills you currently possess, and begin the process of moving toward that worthwhile goal. Will your inner voice be an obstacle, telling you that you cannot accomplish the task? Probably! So don't listen to it: tell yourself *yes I can* and move forward.

Sad to say, most people will never achieve the worthwhile goals they dream of due to a lack of confidence. They will spend their lives never winning any races along the way.

You may be thinking that I am describing you—if so, you must understand that I am only describing you up until *now*. Not the future. At any time, you can make the decision to be a person who understands that *yes you can*.

Take stock of your skills, knowledge, and previous experiences and continue down that path leading to your worthwhile goal. Or you can make up endless excuses as to why you cannot possibly accomplish said goal, and shrink back into your comfort zone like a frightened turtle; it's your choice!

The goal is to live a life of excitement by *Expecting Awesome Daily*. Dreams were put in your head for a reason. So travel down that path and be the person you were destined to be.

In a Nutshell

To live in a reality where we *Expect Awesome Daily*, we must come to the realization that *yes we can*. We must accept the fact that we already possess everything we need for ultimate success. We have to stop listening to that small, sometimes negative, inner voice and understand that we are not as trapped as we believe ourselves to be. We need to stop second-guessing ourselves and realize that we are a lot more prepared than we give ourselves credit for.

Our worthwhile dreams are in our head for a reason. It's time to stop thinking about them—I know you have done enough of that—and stop the procrastination cycle. Move forward because you can!

Helpful Exercise

Doubt, albeit harmful, is a natural human emotion. We should work hard to believe in our abilities because we are far more resilient than we give ourselves credit for.

Make a decision today about something in your life where you have been selling yourself short. What can you step up to the plate for today? Trust in your ability!

Where I've Been Selling Myself Short: _____

_____

What Action I Will Take Today: _____

_____

*Life is better when you have confidence in yourself;
you are stronger than you think!*

Your faith can move mountains—your doubts can create them.

Unknown

Chapter Six

DON'T BE YOUR OWN OBSTACLE

DURING THE SUMMER OLYMPICS, one of the most-watched events is the 100-metre dash. The hurdles race, albeit somewhat similar, doesn't seem to have the same interest draw. Metaphorically speaking, life is closer to the hurdles race than the 100-metre dash; life tends to have some obstacles.

As we travel down our life paths, we will sometimes linger on the challenges placed in our way, often to the point of spending too much time assessing this inconvenient intruder. We ask ourselves: "Did I cause this? Is this my fault?"

It would be unrealistic to expect all our goals to be achieved in one, quick sprint to the finish line. Better, instead, to take the mindset of a hurdler.

To start with, I'm quite sure a hurdler does not look through all 10 hurdles between them and the finish line and bemoan the fact that those 10 obstacles are in the way. Sure, it would be more convenient if they weren't there, but that's the race: hurdle 10 obstacles as quickly as possible and beat everyone else to the finish line.

A hurdler is also not going to stop at each hurdle and evaluate them. They are not going to pause and think, "Do I deserve this? Is this my fault? Am I a victim?" No. They would fly over that challenge with speed and attack the next one with the same vigour, because each one brings them closer to their ultimate goal.

It's common for a hurdler to clip the top of a hurdle as they drive past it. There is no penalty for this: they are past it whether they clipped it or not. Like life, the point in the end is to get over the obstacle and to the finish line.

The path to achieving our goals are just like this: we begin at the starting point, we need to get to the finish line, and natural mishaps are along the way. For an Olympic hurdler, the whole process will take under 15 seconds. For us, our journey could take weeks, months, or even years. However, the process is still the same: it's a hurdle race, not a sprint. Obstacles will be encountered, and they must be conquered.

Just like it's okay for a hurdler to come in contact with the hurdle, it's also okay for you to periodically get tangled up. At that point, you just need to free yourself and keep moving forward. There's no penalty, provided you get past the hurdle.

When you encounter an obstacle, do yourself a favour: skip all the wasteful over-thinking and evaluating. Just leap over it and run on to your next challenge. This will bring you all the closer to your desired result.

It's amazing how many times a client will reach out to me when they reach an obstacle in their path. The amazing part isn't that they reached out, but that they are thinking of packing it in. My response is always the same: "What did you think was going to happen? Did you think it was going to be smooth sailing to every goal?"

There is no doubt that, at times, everything will go your way. And for sure, when that happens to you, that's awesome—enjoy it.

For those who love sailing, you'll know that the waters are calm most of the time, but it's not always that way. There will be times when your skills as a sailor will be tested. Every sailor knows that, if you embark on a long trip, there will be times of calm and times of turmoil; it can't go any other way. For the sailor, this trip is not a 100-metre sprint: it's a hurdle race. Obstacles will be in your way, and your sailing skills will be tested.

In our quest to *Expect Awesome Daily*, one of the biggest detractors is mentally getting bogged down with a challenge. Don't spend too much time lingering on your most recent, unwanted visitor. Handle it instead the way a hurdler would: it's an obstacle standing in your way, so jump over it.

In a hurdle race there are 10 hurdles: every racer is aware of this. Now, I can't say how many hurdles will be on your path, but I can say there will be some. For the sake of illustration, let's just say there are also 10, like a hurdle race. Therefore, the plan is to move as quickly as you can: leaping over the first, on to the second, and so on to complete the race. If you clip a couple on the way, or even them all, don't worry: there is no penalty for that.

To *not be your own obstacle*, you must understand two things:

The First:
We don't want to make things worse by camping out at each hurdle. "But it's not my fault Rob!" you say. I get that the hurdles are not the hurdlers' fault; they're just there. But we need to get past them either way. Of course, it's true that not all the challenges we experience along the way are our own doing. I get that: I really

do. However, that's not the point: we need to get past them and move along.

When a situation has bogged us down, whether it is our doing or not, we have *become our own obstacle*. Nothing good can come from stewing. So put that item in the rear-view mirror as quickly as possible and run on to your next challenge.

The Second:
If we know that hurdles already exist, then let's not intentionally create more to add to life's path. If your path has 10 hurdles, quickly and efficiently overcome them. Complete the process and reap the rewards. Don't add 5 more hurdles to the situation; that just makes the course that much more challenging to complete.

You might wonder why someone would consciously do so. But people do it all the time, actually; it's a lot more common than you might think.

If you are adding obstacles to your path of achievement, then you are, in fact, in your own way; you are the architect of your own demise. Instead, accept life's natural obstacles: leap over them with grace and eliminate the temptation to add additional ones. Fly over most, clip a few, and move aggressively toward the goal that awaits you at the finish line.

Obstacles Are Mostly Imagined

I'm not saying that obstacles are not real: of course they are. I'm just saying that, in most cases, our stumbling blocks stem from our imagination. For some reason, we make up stories and place them squarely in our path. This has created an obstacle that requires energy, focus, and commitment to overcome. A better course of action would have been to not place that object in your path to begin with.

There is no way to accurately determine how many of our challenges are natural and how many we have placed in our own way. However, with more than 20 years of coaching, I feel it is safe to say that the vast majority have been unnecessarily created.

On our quest to experiencing awesome daily, additional challenges will serve no benefit. We are not our own obstacle when conquering life's naturally-occurring challenges, but we are when we have been forced to invest our most valuable asset, time, in overcoming a self-made obstacle.

Because life is a hurdle race, not a sprint, obstacles will be in your way; that's life. The trick is to handle them quick and efficiently. Run to your goal instead of spending unnecessary effort overcoming self-made challenges.

Don't Listen to Others All the Time

There is no doubt that others can be, and are, an amazing source of knowledge and inspiration; I would like to think that I am one of those people. Over the years, my company has guided thousands of individuals down the path of success. And in my own life, many have provided that same service to me. Most are aware of their contribution, but some may not be.

In your life, people will be available to assist you when difficulties arise. Perhaps that person is someone you know personally, or maybe your answer lies in a book, podcast, or some other form of multimedia information. Either way, guidance isn't too far away.

What I wish to do here is caution you on where and how you receive your information. Not all of the advice coming your way is harmful; however, a large percentage will not serve you well. It's quite common in our program for a client to become frustrated when one of our coaches is guiding them in one direction, but they are also getting advice from somewhere else.

Guidance designed to get you over a hurdle is good, but additional advice, even from a well-meaning individual, is the advice that should be ignored.

It's also common for opinions from others to come from a position of envy. These, of course, hold no value for you at all. I'm not saying to put up barriers and ignore guidance. However, you'll want to learn how to recognize the proper advice and implement it immediately.

For those who are giving you bad advice—whether their intention is pure or not—smile, thank them for their input, and don't give it another thought. Not everyone is put on this planet to help you! Don't listen to everyone.

Life is Short

This particular point really sums up why I do what I do. I write from my lake house, so as I write I have an unobstructed view of the lake. People often ask me why I don't just pack it in and live here fulltime; to be honest, sometimes I don't have an answer. It's a really good idea: I love the outdoors, and there is no shortage of things to do there. In fact, it's often difficult to focus on writing when I could be partaking in an amazing outdoor activity.

At the end of the day, life is short: for me as well as everyone else. I have a tremendous passion to assist others in maximizing their lives, which explains why I do what I do. I feel that if I can help others travel down their desired path, I've done my job. If I can play even a small part in assisting others to *Expect Awesome Daily*, I feel like I have made a positive contribution.

I should be clear: I'm not a workaholic by any stretch of the imagination. Life is short, so I live at the lake half the time and enjoy it. I don't manufacture unnecessary obstacles, because I don't want to waste the time to overcome them. And nor should you.

Assume Things Will Run Smoothly

I am a little surprised sometimes by the way people spin things in their head. When they describe to me how a situation could go wrong, I find myself often saying, "Okay, but you could just as easily assume it will go right instead."

Every day in every situation we have a choice: we can assume things will go our way, or we can spin it so that we believe they will work against us. But whichever way you choose, you will end up correct at the end of the day. You become what you think; not what you are supposed to think, or what you are going to think in the future. Only what you think now. In fact, knowing better has no bearing. You need to move in the right direction, and you need to be focussed, period.

Expecting awesome things to happen every day is a wonderful state of mind. Assuming things will run smoothly goes a long way toward creating that mindset. Accidently assuming that nothing will go your way becomes quite the stumbling block.

To live believing that problems are always just around the corner will render you incapable of *Expecting Awesome Daily*. Instead of living every precious day in expectation of something awesome happening, you will unnecessarily be on guard for obstacles that probably don't exist. *You become your own obstacle.*

When You Point

It's so easy to blame others for our misfortunes; however, we need to remember that when we point one finger out, three fingers point back. It can be difficult to take responsibility, and the average person isn't very good at it. This is an aspect of our lives that we can all work to improve.

If our first reaction is to blame those around us for our circumstances, we will miss the opportunity of personal growth: the chance to assess those three fingers back. What part did we play in this scenario? If all we can do is constantly blame others for our perceived misfortune and take none of the responsibility upon ourselves, then our growth process will be painfully slow. I'm not saying that circumstances are constantly our fault; I'm not saying that at all. But to continually blame others is a mistake, one that poses the potential to cost us dearly.

A healthy approach is to consider the part we played in the dilemma we currently face. It's possible that, after careful consideration, it's honestly concluded that we played no part in it. It's equally possible that, perhaps, we were the partial architect of the current hurdle that is in need of conquering.

If we intend to live a life that spends every day *Expecting Awesome*, it's not helpful to constantly hold others as 100% responsible for all our setbacks. If we do, we will be squarely in our own way. So do yourself a favour and free yourself up to move forward.

Remember: when you point one finger out, three fingers point back!

What Are You Meant to Do?

This is a difficult question to understand, and in turn, a difficult one to answer; not because we can't think it through, but because there are so many variables it's challenging to comprehend.

When a river flows to an ocean, it commonly forms a delta upon its arrival. Life paths are like that also. Let's say you set the goal to hit a certain business achievement. For now, it's all you think about. You are like a river, flowing toward the ocean's open water. Although it may not be in a straight line, you have a singular direction: the ocean.

Before a river arrives, a delta will manifest. The river enters the ocean through a number of locations, none of which it was privy to until it occurred. Like the river, you move with vigour toward your goal. But then, without notice, the delta will take place. You have choices to split your attention between. Although they travel in multiple directions, all of them support your ultimate desire.

Success is like that: we travel for quite a while in our focussed direction, and then, seemingly without notice, the delta presents itself. I'm giving you good news here: all of our new choices are in the direction of our goal.

When I started selling real estate in the late 1980's, my goal was clear: sell lots of homes and make a quality life for my family. It really was that simple. My metaphorical river flowed toward the ocean. Of course it meandered a bit, but it always moved in the direction of my end goal: the ocean.

For many years it went that way. Lots of sales meant a quality lifestyle, filled with periodic acknowledgements of my achievements.

In the beginning, my motive was clear and honest: make a good life. Then, one day, I made it to the delta, and new opportunities presented themselves: good, healthy opportunities.

In the beginning, I had no idea that I would train and coach realtors, or own one of the largest real estate coaching and training companies in North America. I wasn't aware that I would teach seminars or, for that matter, write books. I just enjoyed the process of flowing down the river, experiencing an awesome life.

The thing about the delta is that it always happens close to your destination: it's not a midway experience. So it would have been a shame if I spent my entire career meandering in the river, never getting close to the ocean. I never would have experienced (or even been aware of) what was available to me in the delta.

The question to ask yourself is: "What am I meant to do?" What experiences are you meant have? And what opportunities will open up for you? Personally, I'm glad I worked my way down the river; I hope you do the same. Don't get me wrong; I'm not saying that I have arrived. And nor will you, when the delta presents itself; after all, then there is a whole ocean to explore!

Don't be one of those people who say "This is good enough for me," and spend your entire life on the wrong side of the delta. Do yourself a favour: discover what you were meant to do. Then, and only then, will you be living a life *Expecting Awesome Daily*.

Rise Above

The life that you really want must exist above mediocrity. It takes place at a higher level: a level that is free from life's unnecessary distractions. To be clear, I'm not saying that you can eliminate all unwanted circumstances. I'm saying that unnecessary ones can, and should, be eliminated.

Rise above. Guide yourself to a mind free of imagined obstacles;

deal only with those that occur naturally in life. Purposefully live every day *Expecting Awesome*. Purposefully rise above it all: get out of your own way, and live the life you were intended to live.

I can tell you unequivocally that this process will not happen on its own; you need to do your part in this equation. Ask yourself an honest question: is this challenge I'm facing really an issue, or am I making it an issue? Is this something that is going to make a difference in my life, or am I misallocating my valuable resources? Am I living in mediocrity, and stressing over something that should have been allocated to the "not important" category?

If so, allow yourself to rise above it all and live on a higher level. This is necessary if you are serious about your life goals.

I can't really tell you what percentage of your challenges are valid and which are fabricated—or, at least, elevated beyond an appropriate level. In this way, each person is different. However, I can confidently say that each and every one of us spends way too much of our valuable time managing challenges that should have been allocated as unimportant.

This book is about *Expecting Awesome Daily* as a normal train of thought. It goes without saying that spending too much time getting worked up over minor issues becomes an obvious stumbling block. So intentionally attack life's naturally-occurring challenges head-on. Leap over those that, in the big picture, don't make a tangible difference.

In a Nutshell

It's important that we are not our own obstacles. Clear a path from those hurdles you create so that you can *Expect Awesome Daily*. Life is short, so it's important that we live our lives in a way that allows us to experience all the wonders that are available. Or you can choose to travel through a life of mediocrity: most do.

If a motorcycle is available, I don't think you should purposefully choose to get around on a bicycle; however, that is exactly what the vast majority of people do.

We do have a choice: assume things will run smoothly, and correctly allocate those unimportant events so that they do not bog you down. Move past them with minimal energy expended.

Don't be your own obstacle. Take a moment to get out of our own way and experience life at its fullest. Trade shackles for wings!

Helpful Exercise

In this exercise, I would like you to identify an obstacle that has you effectively stuck. Maybe you have been stationary in achieving this goal for some time, or maybe this obstacle has recently captured you; either way, you are effectively immobilized. Write it down. Analyze it: is it something that should be considered less important than it currently is? Release yourself from its control.

Obstacle that is Currently Holding Me Back: _____

What is Stopping Me: _____

Is This Obstacle as Important as I Think it Is? _____

Affirmation: _____ I am done I am moving on!

In the Olympics, professional hurdlers don't spend any time on each hurdle—they just fly right over them.
I would suggest you do the same!

If you find a path with no obstacles, it probably doesn't lead anywhere.

Frank Clark

Chapter Seven

CONTROL WHAT YOU CAN

I'M SURE YOU have heard this statement many times: "control what you can and forget the rest." It's good advice, but it's easier said than done.

All situations have two sides: what you can control and what you can't. Trying to manage both sides will only end in frustration, since although one side is our responsibility, the other is under someone else's jurisdiction.

We need to look at how we handle situations in an honest manner: are we correctly dealing with only the side of the situation that is our responsibility, or are we trying to control both sides of the equation? Because one of those sides is outside of our influence. We would serve ourselves much better to spend time on what we *can* control and less, if any, on that which we cannot.

As an example, let's say you are seeking new employment. You can't make the person hire you. You can, however, control your side of the equation by upgrading your education in a manner that makes you more employable.

In a marriage, whenever one person attempts to control both sides of the relationship, you've already got a problem on your hands. The only part you can control is how you choose to make yourself the best possible partner. Hopefully, your partner will have the same attitude, allowing you to achieve a harmonious union.

In our desire to spend our days *Expecting Awesome,* we must let go of what we clearly cannot control. Instead, we should refocus all our efforts on what we can, in fact, manage: our side of the situation.

Take Small Steps

When we take any path toward a worthwhile goal, it's important to embrace a patient mindset. Although it is important that we arrive at our goal, it should be pointed out that we don't need to arrive today—or even in the next couple of days. Everything takes time, so it's important that we are patient. Impatience has the potential to derail our forward progress.

A tangible solution is to break down our goal into manageable pieces. These smaller steps can then be taken and dispensed of in short order. I observe many clients as they set worthwhile goals in order to live their life at a more fulfilling level. Unfortunately, without some guidance, their odds of success are minimal. This is because, in their aspirations to be better, they do not first break down their goal into manageable pieces.

There are several benefits to this method and its subsequent processing procedure. The first is that it's simply easier. Losing some weight is a great example. Perhaps your current weight is

180lbs, and your ideal weight is 160lbs.

First we'll want to break it up into smaller steps: perhaps 5lb increments. Let's say you have given yourself four months to achieve this goal. So at the end of Month One, you should be at 175lbs, then 170lbs at Month Two, and so on. This is a lot easier to stick to versus solely focussing on being 160lbs four months from now.

This approach will also prevent us from falling into the common procrastination trap that derails most worthwhile goals. When we embark on a goal that has a future completion date, our brains automatically assume in the beginning that we have lots of time; there's no hurry to get started.

In this case, let's say that on January 1st you set the goal to be 160lbs by April 31st. Because the finish date is so far in the future, it would be easy to think, *No hurry right now; I have lots of time.*

On the other hand, let's consider that same goal in the identical time frame (160lbs by April 31st), but in this scenario the goal setter was wise and understood the importance of breaking their goal into manageable steps. They commence on January 1st thinking, *First stop, 175lbs by January 31st—no time to waste!*

I've noticed in coaching that, when clients set a goal for their year, they are lackadaisical in the early weeks. Fortunately, we are well aware of what takes place, seeing as our planet is plagued with procrastination. The procrastination mindset is, *Relax, it's January; you have all year to hit your goal.* This results in the client getting behind and playing the unfortunate game of catch-up all year.

As a solution to the tricks our brains play on such long-term goals, we have our clients break their annual goals down into four, 90-day cycles. There is a lot more urgency in their spirit when their focus is squarely committed to being at a certain point by March 31st instead of December 31st.

Considering that *Expecting Awesome Daily* is purely a matter of mindset, attacking smaller, worthwhile goals makes it a lot easier to stay on track. When we get off-track, our mind goes to an unproductive place, rendering it difficult to notice the awesome events milling about on a regular basis.

Breaking your goals down into bite-sized chunks will eliminate mental lapses, so that you can better understand what you need to control and when. However, I can unequivocally say that not only will the smaller steps approach be easier for you, you will also be off-track much less, creating a better mindset overall.

Small Senses of Accomplishment

Breaking our goals into smaller steps also allows us to experience small senses of accomplishment as we complete them and move ourselves closer to our overall goal.

Let's revisit our example of a person focussed on weighing in at a lean, mean, 160lbs. Currently, at 180lbs, their motivation is all about what they're trying to avoid: a closet full of clothes where nothing fits or feels right.

When their scale flashes up 175lbs on February 1st, it's time to celebrate: mission accomplished. And don't under-estimate that small sense of accomplishment. The last thing their brain wants to do now is to give it back. Their motivation is now about what they are trying to keep: the lost weight and that definitive step closer to their goal.

That said, the line to an accomplished goal is never a straight one: there is always some meandering. It should be noted that when our mind experiences that first little accomplishment (and the subsequent unwillingness to give it back), it will still periodically relent and relinquish some of its gains.

So although it's not perfect, I can tell you that when your brain desperately wants to hold onto its profits, it will meander a lot less. We can't control the meandering, but we can control our mindset. This will assist you in achieving your worthwhile goal.

Alternatively, consider your path if we were to eliminate all those little senses of accomplishment. Your brain would not be as determined to hold onto its gains, because it won't see them as something completed. I'm not saying you won't hit your goal—perhaps you will. I'm just saying that your path will have a lot more meandering.

These unnecessary twists and turns that use your valuable resources are obstacles you were the architect of. And thus they are obstacles that you can control. Take the path of least resistance: *control what you can* and move forward. Enjoy the small senses of accomplishment as each section is transferred to the completed side of the to-do list.

Life is a journey. Break it into small, manageable pieces and enjoy the process.

Always Advance

Success is never a straight line. Some say it should be in a perfect world, but should it really? It is said we learn more from our mistakes than from our successes. I'm a believer in that philosophy. What's important isn't that we don't make mistakes: it's that we are always moving in the direction of our goal.

The road to accomplishment is a meandering path. In travelling it, you will take in some sights, experiences, and activities that were not originally on the manifest.

Consider a rope that is 10ft long. If you stretch it in a straight line and measure it, it will have covered 10ft of distance. If you wiggle the rope left and right a couple times and then measure your distance, perhaps only 4ft will have been covered. The rope, of course, is still 10ft in length. However, due to its meandering route, only 4ft were covered. Striving to achieve goals is closer to this example than the straight line.

We can't control the meandering path. However, how we choose to process the path will dictate our outcome of success or failure. Most would prefer the direct line, and will thus abandon the worthwhile goal when faced with a meandering route. Personally, I do not prefer the direct line, which is convenient for me, seeing as that rarely happens.

I accept with open arms that the non-direct route is the path that holds all the unexpected experiences, some of which are life-changing. Personal growth lies in these unexpected situations. After the fact, you may find that you would not change these situations for the world.

Don't get me wrong: occasionally, I embark on a goal and, for whatever reason, that goal is accomplished, quick and simple. I'm okay with experiencing a straight line scenario; it happens sometimes. However, I do wonder about the experiences that went undiscovered: perhaps the people I would have met, or the off-the-beaten-path locations my straight line avoided. I'll still take it—why not—but given the choice, I would prefer the adventure of the meandering path.

We learn things when we end up in a location that was not part of our original route. And it's this location that lies to the left or right that a straight line to success would have avoided. But these are the stops that add depth and substance to our lives.

I do like flying directly to a new location, but nothing beats a road trip full of undiscovered adventure. I think all too often we get so focussed on getting to where we want to be that we miss the adventure of personal growth along the way.

Thus the trick to ensure you are always moving in the direction of your goal, whether your path is meandering or not, is to *always advance*.

You can't control the path, but you can control what you do on it. Stop and smell the roses occasionally. Awesome things are always happening around you, so make sure that you are not so focussed on walking the straight line that you are missing out on the wonderful experiences available to you just a smidgen to the left or right.

Either way the goal is accomplished. Both are good, but if I had my way, I would take the adventure all day long.

As a business coach, it's my job to assist individuals in achieving their goals. My work days are spent involved in conversations about their journeys, mostly with those that take the meandering route. In them, I always point out the adventure they are experiencing.

At first, they usually think I'm kidding or using some sort of mind-over-matter technique, but I'm not. I'm simply pointing out that, in this case, the rare, straight line is not at work. Instead, the much-sought-after meandering path has presented itself.

I encourage the client to do themselves a favour and enjoy the process, because there are going to be some exciting adventures along the way; it would be a shame to possess the incorrect mindset and miss out on them.

It's important to realize that the goal will still be accomplished. It will probably take a little more time—after all, you are visiting a few more destinations and having a few extra experiences.

I often ask people why they're in such a rush all the time. I'm all for setting goals and accepting the occasional straight line; however, the unexpected experiences are where the fun is. You can't control the unexpected, so just keep moving forward and enjoy the process.

Do Your Part

Everyone wants to be able to *Expect Awesome Daily;* of course that's a given. One of the key saboteurs of this desired state of mind is mistakenly thinking that you can control both sides of a situation. But you can only do your part and control your side.

In relationships, this mistake is a common one: one of the two will try to control both themselves and their partner. I'm not saying that they can't stay together, but it would be difficult for the relationship to remain harmonious and the couple to experience fulfillment. Clearly I'm no marriage counsellor, but I think you get my point that it would be better if both just did their part and let their partner handle their own side.

This applies to any situation, be it a relationship, a business endeavour, or a personal goal. Either way, your responsibility is to manage your side of the equation. You would be wise to spend more of your efforts squarely focussed on your responsibility; let others handle theirs.

Some people would say, "Sure Rob, that sounds great—but what if the other person isn't doing their part?" I agree that it is unfortunate; however, if you are honest with yourself, you would see that when you tried to pick up the slack of someone else's irresponsibility in the past, your extra efforts were probably in vain. They may have even made the situation worse.

Do yourself a favour and spend your time on your side of the equation. Don't try to make up for what you perceive as someone else's shortcoming. Attempting to control both sides of a situation is an *Expecting Awesome* killer!

Be Patient

It's been said that patience is a virtue. For that reason, when I ask clients if they are patient people, they all respond in the affirmative. But as we work with clients, we realize that quite the opposite tends to play out.

I do wonder sometimes why everyone seems to be in such a hurry. Everything takes time. We all know how life plays out: hopefully we live to a ripe old age; however, that is not guaranteed. What is guaranteed is that we pass on.

It seems to me that far too many people are in a hurry to get to the end. Life is not about work, work, work and only then enjoy the golden years. What if the golden years never come—what if a shorter life is in the cards for you?

Life is about enjoying the journey: the adventure of day in and day out, and finding yourself in interesting situations as you travel your chosen road. If you are fortunate enough to enjoy those amazing golden years, what a blessing. But wouldn't it be great if life were exciting all along the way instead of just those final years? I'm just saying I notice a lot of people who focus on the future, and not enough on the amazing now. You can have it all!

In our journey we should assume the best: plan for a long, adventurous lifetime filled with exciting twists and turns. But along those twists and turns, patience is going to come into play on a regular basis.

Whenever we encounter an unexpected twist, patience will be required. Sometimes, in our desire to get around a perceived setback, a lack of patience is expressed. But this only serves to further elongate our frustration. Patience is the correct approach. In fact, in exercising patience you might just find a valuable learning experience, or perhaps even the hidden gem of an enjoyable surprise.

Human beings are wired to achieve; it explains why we have been around for so long. It's true that many have misplaced their zest for achievement; however, that doesn't mean that it cannot be rekindled.

Patience is a key ingredient in many of the success principles. In order to have a determined spirit, patience will be required. A life of passion cannot be achieved without exercising patience on a regular basis. I could go on: so trust me when I say that, without patience, you will not experience the same level of success.

When a worthwhile goal is abandoned, unfortunately a lack of patience is often one of the culprits. It's not always the only culprit, but it is almost always present. Lack of patience really has no benefit; things take time, so don't rob yourself of all the amazing scenery along the way.

In our quest to live a life of *Expecting Awesome Daily*, being patient becomes a frustration-remover. Life is better with patience, not to mention a lot more fun. Frustration is sometimes inevitable, so you might as well not add to it!

So when you're feeling impatient, ask yourself: "What's my hurry?" Relax and enjoy the ride.

Completion Isn't the Only Accomplishment

Of course it is amazing when a worthwhile goal is achieved: you get that immense sense of satisfaction that goes along with an accomplished goal. Not to take away from that amazing feeling, but it can, and should, be made much bigger than that by giving yourself many smaller senses of accomplishment.

Let's say you have a goal to expand your business and earn yourself 20 new clients. Of course, once you've met this goal in full, there will be a tremendous sense of accomplishment.

In fact, that accomplishment would fulfil your *Expected Awesome* for the day. If someone asked you, "How was your day today?" your answer to that question would definitely be, "Awesome. I made another new client and met my goal for the term. Now I'm no longer worried about how my business will expand."

If you shared that awesome news with me, I would be sincerely happy for you, and impressed that you saw the process through to completion: that in and of itself is amazing. But I would hope that many smaller senses of accomplishment were present along the way. If gathering 20 new clients took a year to come to fruition, a great idea would be to break the 20 clients into smaller numbers: perhaps 4 instances of 5 new clients.

If the timeline allocated for the entire process was one year, that would mean you could easily earn 5 new clients every 90 days. With this approach, we pick up a couple of benefits:

Firstly

Our goal appears easier to accomplish. Mentally, we focus on the 5 clients instead of the entire 20, which could be seen as daunting. With 5 new clients at the 90-day point, we have another awesome event taking place. This approach gives us 3 additional senses of accomplishment along the way, as well as the big feeling upon completion.

It would be a great idea to reward yourself with each step achieved along the way. It doesn't have to be extravagant: something small, but notable. Your goal is work-related, so maybe something fun to celebrate the partial completion of your worthwhile goal.

Secondly

Breaking goals into smaller pieces is simply easier, much easier. This fact has been proven many times over in regard to achieving goals. Your brain has a much simpler time with smaller tasks, and so the odds of getting bogged down are greatly reduced.

You are *controlling what you can*: this includes how you view your goal. The goal itself doesn't change; nor do the circumstances around it. But you have controlled how you view that goal for the better.

If you intend to live in a constant mental state of *Expecting Awesome Daily*, what could be better than breaking down your goals into smaller tasks? You're creating your own awesome events on a regular basis.

In a Nutshell

While I work with people on their quests to better their lives, I find that in most cases they try to control a lot more than they are responsible for. If you choose this route, you are purposefully choosing a path of frustration.

Clients often debate with me on this point. They do their best to sell me on why they need to control both sides of a situation: "You don't understand, Rob; the other player isn't doing their part." I get that: I really do. However, that doesn't change the process: you can only control your side of the equation.

Your job is to be patient. Take small steps and keep moving in the right direction. The goal of this book is to assist individuals in living every day in an honest state of *Expecting Awesome Daily*. Do yourself a favour: *control what you can* and leave the rest alone. Be patient and move with small steps toward your ultimate goal.

Helpful Exercise

Identify one situation in your life where you have made the mistake of trying to control a part that is clearly not your responsibility.

This is My Situation: _____

This is the Side of the Situation That is My Responsibility to Control: _____

This is the Side of the Situation That is Not My Responsibility to Control: _____

I Have Been Over-Stepping My Bounds in This Area: _____
_____

Starting Today, I Will Let This Situation Go. It Is Not My Responsibility.

If you are trying to control an area that is not your responsibility, you are probably—no, definitely—only making it worse!

All I can control is myself and just keep having a positive attitude.

Rose Namajunas

Chapter Eight

EMBRACE

IN OUR QUEST to *Expect Awesome Daily*, it's paramount that we acquire the ability to *embrace* both positive and negative situations. Vigorously embracing those daily positive occurrences is easy; everyone is good at that. The trick, of course, is to hold fast to all of life's gems. It should be noted that some scenarios that have been deemed unwanted probably possess some, if not a lot, of benefit.

I wouldn't say embrace everything in life; of course opportunities arise that could potentially take us in an undesirable direction. I give you the credit to recognize those dangerous paths. However, positive opportunities should obviously be immediately latched onto, while the undesirable, or even dangerous, ones should be identified and rejected.

Sometimes, though, a situation will arise that cannot be immediately allocated to the obvious positive or personally damaging paths. Often, that item will possesses value in that there is something to be learned from it. Therefore, if your visitor is not damaging to the different aspects of your life, you should *embrace* it as welcome.

As an example, let's say your boss calls you into their office to inform you that your work effort has not gone unnoticed. Therefore, a promotion with an increase in pay and responsibility will be effective immediately. This opportunity is immediately recognizable as a positive one.

On the other hand, what if the meeting were to play out this way: your boss acknowledges the skills you bring to the table, and is impressed with a few aspects of your work. They view you as a valuable part of the team, but have questions about a couple of areas of your contribution.

In the first scenario, it's easy to embrace that meeting; I'm sure you would view that as your awesome event for the day. But I wonder how you would react to the second meeting. If you came home from work and someone asked you how your day was, would you say, "Awesome, I had a great meeting today with my boss. They pointed out a few areas I can work on to set me up for future advancement in the company." Or would you say, "My boss was on my case again—nothing seems to make them happy"?

Truth be told, there is tremendous value in the second meeting. The person living their life in search of awesome things daily would recognize that it wasn't wholly negative. The question you have to ask yourself is: do you possess the mental fortitude to view this information as beneficial? Most people would focus on the perceived negative portion of the conversation, and thus miss out on the positive opportunity for advancement in the future.

You might think that living in this state of mind is not realistic. But in fact, it is quite practical. It is simply the route a person will take once they have been purposefully *Expecting Awesome Daily* for an extended period of time.

These situations we perceive as obstacles can just as easily be spun to be beneficial. I realize that this line of thinking is not the most common on our planet; however, I think you would agree that the vast majority of people are not consciously spending their time to search for something awesome. If they were, then this behaviour would become much more common.

Being on the search for daily awesome events could be the norm for you. Find the good in everything.

When our children misbehave, they don't like the consequences. However, those consequences are necessary and quite often beneficial for the child; they don't see it, but it's there. In some ways, we are still that child.

Everything takes time; in most cases, a lot more time than we had originally budgeted for. When that happens, how we spin things in our brains makes all the difference in the world. We can look at things from the perspective of "Gosh this is taking a long time; I was expecting a direct route." Or we can buckle up, settle in, and enjoy the ride.

Consider these two viewpoints over the course of a lifetime. If we're always trying to get somewhere in a hurry, then when life is over it's as if we spent our lives impatiently trying to get somewhere and never arriving.

On the other hand, the person who has purposefully taken the patient approach has appreciated the meandering ride, taken in the extra sights, and enjoyed some unexpected experiences. Personally, I'm really grateful that the straight line to accomplishing a worthwhile goal is rare. Things do take time: it's important to *embrace* that fact and enjoy the process. Everything experienced along the way has value.

In my line of work, it's common for me to observe people in a great hurry to get somewhere. I point out to them that none of us are going to get out of this life alive—so why are they in such a hurry to get to the end? Shouldn't they be doing their best to slow down and enjoy the process, since we all know how it will end?

I need to be clear: this book is about living a life squarely focussed on *Expecting Awesome Daily*. I'm not saying you should grin and bear the fact that those worthwhile goals you have set are going to occasionally take longer than you had planned. I'm saying we need to *embrace* that fact.

When something is accomplished quickly, of course embrace it. However, that should not be your preference. When embarking on a worthwhile journey, enjoy the adventurous route. Don't be in a hurry to get to the end—we all know how that's going to wind up.

Decide what success means to you. Chart your course and secretly hope for many unexpected twists and turns. Enjoy the smaller senses of satisfaction they grant well before the substantial accomplishment of a goal well-met.

Embrace the process. Enjoy every day by stopping in new and exciting destinations. Don't be in a hurry to get to the end!

Embrace Others' Achievements

A key factor in being able to maintain a mindset of *Expecting Awesome Daily* is whether you can be sincerely happy for others' achievements. And I don't mean an outward expression of support; I mean a genuine happiness for them when there is no benefit to you. This is something you will have to feel on a personal level, deep within yourself.

If asked, anyone would affirm that "Yes, I am happy when others succeed." However, human nature proves the opposite to be true in most cases.

Let me stress that your outward appearance is not what I'm talking about; most people can achieve that easily. I'm referring to your inner reaction upon learning of another person's success. Perhaps at a dinner party it comes up in conversation. Obviously, a round of praise from you, accompanied with a toast, is normal protocol.

In this case, you have to take a good, long look at your ever-important internal reaction. I'm quite sure you would outwardly partake in the appropriate accolades. The question is, does your inner opinion match your outward behaviour?

This becomes one of those unexpected little pleasures of life—enjoying what others have achieved as well as what you have. If you are in such a hurry to get down your own path, someone else's achievements will only serve to irritate you. This is a character flaw, one that will rob you of an opportunity to live *Expecting Awesome Daily*.

Embracing the success of others is the much better path. The opposite is a path that leads to one of the biggest dream killers: envy.

Every Cloud Has a Silver Lining

"Every cloud has a silver lining" is more than just a catchy saying: it's a truth that you should incorporate into your daily thinking process. There is good in almost everything.

Yes, it's true that situations fall onto the positive or the perceived negative side of the ledger, but the silver lining is still present. It is easy to identify those that reside on the positive side. For those that fall on the initial unwanted side, the silver lining will require some searching.

It's unfortunate, but also true that many people get too engrossed in circumstances that they perceive as negative. This builds mentally on the "why me?" line of thinking, rendering the silver lining virtually undiscoverable.

Life's moments of personal growth come in many different shapes and sizes; it would be limiting to think that only those circumstances we initially processed as positive hold any value. If your experiences are split 50/50 (half being interpreted as positive and the remaining half as negative), then a lot of them would be tossed away in the "why me?" line of thinking. We must *embrace* everything that falls into our life's path.

As a business coach, the most common conversation I can have with a client is probably about maximizing their life. In their quest, I observe all of their frustration when things don't perfectly go their way. I do experience their highs when they have what they perceive as a win, but the other half, those events that they perceive as a loss, are in some cases lamented rather than embraced.

I do my best to explain that all situations have value; it's a given that the value is easy to find when a win is experienced, and more challenging to identify in a perceived loss. If we really want to spend our lives *Expecting Awesome Daily*, we must *embrace* all of life's twists and turns.

At the end of the day, we do not get a do-over: you only get one shot at this amazing life. As was pointed out to me in a seminar I spoke at, some people believe in reincarnation. But even in that case, you are not coming back as you; the you of right now, in this life, still only has one chance. Whether or not you get another shot as someone or something else is immaterial.

Everyone reading motivational books such as this one have a desire to better themselves. Otherwise, why bother? Novels are more fun and intriguing reads. So if we truly want to improve ourselves, we need to take the time to find the good in all of life's visitors, be they positive or negative. It doesn't make sense to only find satisfaction in those moments that our brain has processed as positive.

So let's hone our personal capability of finding the benefit in every situation. I realize this goes against conventional thinking, but the seven billion people on this planet aren't living their lives focussed on *Expecting Awesome Daily* (yet).

It would be a mistake on our part to expect that our awesome item of the day will always be clothed in what we perceive as a positive situation.

Make an Effort to Spin Things Positively

In our quest to *Expect Awesome Daily*, we must purposefully spin events in our heads in a positive light. It all comes down to a choice, and it's paramount that we make the right one. Our future selves are relying on us.

Through natural conditioning, our minds unfortunately slip to the negative in many instances. When events fall on the positive side of the ledger, of course it's easy to embrace the bright side. Even in neutral situations, spinning things positively can be relatively easy. However, in life there are many scenarios that we may assess as unwanted.

Now, I don't have my head in the sand; of course I am aware that in some situations finding the positive can be exceptionally challenging. But that does not change the point. However challenging to do so, your job is to find that positive aspect.

Take time to give some honest consideration to what I am saying. Consider how strong your mindset will have to be in order to adhere to this type of thinking. Purposefully looking for the silver lining on all of life's events—the positive, neutral, and negative ones—is challenging. But we need to do so in order to have that absolute expectation that something awesome is literally right around the corner. Looking for the positive in everything is an essential piece in the *Expecting Awesome Daily* puzzle.

I realize that you are probably not this dedicated to the spin-positive mindset right now; however, that doesn't mean that you cannot be this dedicated in the future. Start today. Purposefully make an effort to see the silver lining in every cloud. You don't have to go from zero to hero: just get started.

The good news is that every day will give you new scenarios to practise on; in life, there is no shortage of opportunities to learn to embrace.

Be All In

This point is mostly one of mindset. That said, there are some practical steps you can take to render yourself "all in." It's all about attitude: you are either mentally all in or you are not. There isn't really any middle ground.

When communicating with clients, I encounter one of two mindsets with regards to goals: either I observe an unwavering resolve, or I can tell that a person's mind is still in "try" mode. But "try" mode isn't going to cut it. To quote an iconic scene, "Try not! Do ... or do not. There is no try." – Yoda

When assisting clients who are still stuck in "try" mode, I always struggle to find the correct means of communicating to them that their worthwhile goals have very little chance of occurring this way.

On the other hand, with clients who purposefully choose to be all in no matter what, I can confidently assure them that we will reach their desired destination; we may arrive a bit late, but we will arrive.

The choice of whether to say "I'm all in!" or "Well, we'll give it a try and see what happens," is totally in your corner. You are the one who makes this decision, and it will be the difference between success and failure. Seeing as either decision is equally easy to make, purposefully choose the all-in mindset and reap your rewards.

Many years ago, when I was a young man, I managed a warehouse: a reasonably good job for someone in their mid-twenties. When I submitted my resignation, my employer was both disappointed and a little concerned. I had been married a few years and planned to enter the entrepreneurial world. Josh, my oldest, was one, and my wife, Coleen, was pregnant with our second child, Corissa.

From the company's point of view, they were losing a good employee who had potential to advance within the company, and their concern was that with a young, growing family I would be leaving a lot of security in the search of my worthwhile goal. Obviously they had a point. Nevertheless, I was determined: I thanked them for their concern, but I was confident that I was made for greater things.

On my last day, they informed me that if my entrepreneurial escapades didn't work out, there would always be a job for me with them. Most people would consider that a blessing, and I did appreciate their offer. However, I knew having that knowledge in

Embrace

the back of my mind would prevent me from being all in.

So I thanked them for their kind gesture and said, "Please give my job away, and if I ever walk through that door again, call security." We laughed a bit; they understood exactly where I was coming from.

I needed to cut the rope and eliminate Plan B. 100% of my focus had to remain on my new endeavour. If I knew that I could pull the plug at any time, it would have played out negatively for my aspirations.

That pleasant exchange was 32 years ago, and to this day I have not set foot back in that warehouse. If I did, I'm not sure they wouldn't still call security!

That company had genuine intentions when they offered me a security net; however, that net probably would have caused me to fail. I can vividly remember some challenges that I faced early on: if I wasn't all in, I might have taken the net.

Whatever you try to accomplish, you will be required to be mentally all in. A practical step to assist you in your mental preparedness is to remove your Plan B: be either all in or all out. You can't swim across a river with one foot on the shore!

Embrace the all in attitude and live a life *Expecting Awesome Daily.*

You Are Closer Than You Think

Whenever we aspire to something, regardless of what aspect of our lives it is in, it's common for our brain to sell us on the fact that a massive chasm exists between where we want to be and our current location. Although it may be true that, on occasion, we do need to put in a fair amount of personal development and effort, most of the time this is not the case.

Although it may appear to you that your goal is far away, maybe even unachievable, the truth is you are always closer than you think. In fact, you are probably only a few steps away from making significant headway in the accomplishment of your worthwhile goal.

I have noticed in my years of training realtors that they fall into this trap on a regular basis. Unfortunately, the ramifications of feeling totally lost when you are, in fact, just a few steps from being on track will rob a person of the ability to *Expect Awesome Daily*.

The other day I was speaking to a new coaching client who languished in this unproductive line of thinking. In our first conversation, their desperate tone was extremely evident. So I inquired as to where they were right now and where their desired destination was.

It became clear to me that in their mind they were lost in a metaphorical desert. However, from what I could see, we were only a couple of minor adjustments away from being on the road to achievement.

It goes without saying that this individual was not enjoying the *Expecting Awesome Daily* mindset. They were, in fact, robbed of that luxury due to their incorrect thinking.

Their goal was to assist 20 families in making a move from House A to House B. Not that complicated of a goal, really: they worked in an area with plenty of families doing that exact thing. All they had to do was get involved in the sales that were already happening.

When I shared this with them, their response was, "You make it sound so easy." It kind of was. Rather than buying into the lost-in-the-desert mindset, why not embrace the idea that we're closer than we realize?

Upon inquiring about their recent activities, it became clear that their entire day had been spent stressing about their perceived lost-in-the-desert reality. I suggested instead that they call all of their past clients and inform them of some new market value; people are always interested in that information. During those calls, if they happen to know someone who is thinking about buying or selling, they will probably tell you.

I also suggested looking for some streets where a home had recently sold; neighbours are usually curious about how the house did in regard to price. Why not take an afternoon and have those conversations?

This particular client is a great student and an amazing person; they just accidently got caught up in some negative thinking. Within a couple of weeks, both activities had paid off and they were working with several prospects.

This scenario is really quite common. Any good, hard working person can think that they are lost in the desert when they are, in fact, just a couple of adjustments away from being on track.

When you are on track it is so easy to live each and every day *Expecting Awesome*. On the other hand, when your brain is telling you that you are lost in the desert, living every day expecting awesome events is virtually impossible.

Life is a full-contact sport: there will be times when you are actually lost in the desert. I get that, and I have been there. When the desert is your reality, do your very best and work your way out; don't settle down to live there. People sometimes tell me, "I'm going through hell." I always respond with, "Please don't stop there: keep moving."

In most cases, the lost-in-the-desert thinking is not reality;

it stems from negative imaginings. The trick here is not to dwell: implement a couple of strategies and get back on track.

In most cases, you are closer than you think. Train yourself to look for solutions, and move away from the common lamenting attitude.

In a Nutshell

In order to actively live a life *Expecting Awesome Daily,* it's paramount that we *embrace* the ebb and flow of life. During times of flow, it is easy to embrace positive events. On the other hand, during an ebb the experiences we perceived as negative will prove more challenging to embrace. However, they will still be required.

It's been said that every cloud has a silver lining. I realize that said silver lining can, at times, be well-hidden. An embracing attitude will assist us in our search for whatever aspects are concealed; we will always encounter varied situations as we wind our way through this amazing life.

This chapter is dedicated to Randy Thomas Vivian, one of the few people who is a better fisherman than me. RIP, and God bless.

Helpful Exercise

Both positive and negative circumstances will come your way. Make the decision to embrace one positive and one negative situation that has come your way recently. The circumstance you embrace that occupies the positive side of the ledger will allow you to build upon it. Your conscious decision to embrace any negative visitor will allow you the opportunity to process said circumstance with a much better attitude.

I Embrace This Positive Aspect of My Life: _____
_____

I Embrace This Negative Aspect of My Life: _____
_____

I am not suggesting in any way that by embracing a bona fide negative situation it will be solved. I am saying your new attitude will better equip you with the necessary skills to combat it.

Your life does not get better by chance, it gets better by change.

Jim Rohn

Chapter Nine

WHAT DO YOU HAVE?

IN OUR QUEST to live a life *Expecting Awesome Daily*, it's important that we take stock of what we have. All too often, we incorrectly buy into the idea that we start anything new from scratch.

In some rare cases, it is true that you start from a dead stop. In that case, everything will be new as you endeavour to accomplish your goal. An example is learning a new language: in all likelihood, you begin this process without any previous knowledge. Every step along the way will be a new experience.

Or maybe playing the piano has piqued your interest, but before now music has been a foreign subject to you. In the future, you will be communicating with others who don't know your native tongue and entertaining people with your musical abilities.

So although you will occasionally start from a standstill, most of the time that is not the case. Whenever you embark on a quest of any kind, first take stock of what you currently possess. What attributes or tools already in your possession are going to come in handy as you tackle this newfound adventure?

While working with clients, it's commonly difficult for me to draw this out of them. At first glance, it seems a simple thing: list what attributes you bring to the table. What skills in your possession will be beneficial in achieving what you deem important?

Their common response is, "I don't have anything. I know what I want my life to look like, but unfortunately, I am starting at zero." I know better than to accept this initial assessment. In fact, in most cases they already have part of the solution. I'll have to point out to them that the purpose of being successful, no matter what that means to them, is to push themselves to be better. Not to make a whole new person, but rather a better version of the person who already exists.

I realize human beings desire to excel and move in what we perceive as a positive direction. What we need to realize is that we already possess part of the finished product.

If this weren't true, we would actually be on a quest to create a whole new you. This would be a mistake: you are supposed to be pushing yourself to create a better, more refined you: You 2.0, if you will. I get concerned when people are so unhappy with themselves that they wish to become a whole new person altogether.

Obviously I am a devout supporter of personal growth. I firmly believe in being the best you that you can be. However, I'm opposed to trying to turn yourself into someone you are not; that path is not going to lead to a positive result. Instead, let's take stock of *what you have*, itemize what you need, and chart a course to a better you—not a whole new you. Trust me: you are awesome the way you are.

I realize you are not always where you want to be. However, it would be a mistake on your part if you considered yourself totally lost. The "better you" that you seek is right there on the horizon, so the faster we can get out of the "I'm lost" mode of thinking, the better. You have many qualities, gifts, and attributes.

A natural desire to advance is fine. So let's take stock of *what we have*. Acknowledge that you are not lost. Take a breath, and let's move in a positive direction. You may feel lost, but I can assure you that you are not.

A common mistake the masses make is comparing themselves to others whom they perceive as farther along the path of success. The funny thing is, that is only our perspective. Those people probably consider themselves just as lost when they look at others.

Emulating someone who is genuinely where we want to be is fine; emulating positive role models is very helpful, but comparing ourselves to all others will only serve as a negative influence and become a stumbling block. You may not believe me, but others are watching you and consider you as the one who has it all together

It's vital that, at the end of the day, you are happy with who you are. This is not necessarily being happy with *where* you are; in fact it's quite likely you are not even close to where you would like to be in life. I can empathize with that: I've been there. There is a big difference between not being happy with who you are and not being content with your station in life. Desiring to improve your personal situation is good, helpful, and natural. Not liking who you are is neither good nor helpful.

In my first book, *The Grass is Greener on This Side of the Fence*, I lay out a series of perspective situations that are designed to help you discover that you are okay as you are. If you desire to improve, you must first come to grips with the fact that things are good on this side of the fence prior to venturing over to the other side.

We all rightly want to live *Expecting Awesome Daily*. But constantly viewing our lives as if we are lost will make that mindset virtually impossible to achieve daily.

You Are Closer Than You Think

If only we knew how close we really were to our goals; our lives would be so different. It's been said that most people quit just prior to their breakthrough. Reminding yourself that you are closer than you think is a very helpful way to combat this.

Perhaps you are working your way toward a worthwhile business goal. Before you do so, take stock of the skills you currently possess that will come in handy to reach your ultimate destination. As you travel down the path, learning new skills along the way, there is no doubt some trials await. When they occur, a mantra of "I'm closer than I think" will be very helpful; in fact, it could be the difference between success and failure.

Consistently thinking that you are lost kills your ability to *Expect Awesome Daily*. This is why so few ever achieve greatness. They constantly ignore what they have and their past accomplishments. This only enforces the "woe is me" mindset. Better instead to say "Okay, what do I have? What have I done in the past, and how can I take my current skills and augment them with some new ones?" This will create a more favourable future for you on many different levels. You are closer than you think!

You Are a Unique Individual

We would be wise to spend some time considering our uniqueness.

I know that sometimes on this over-populated planet we can easily consider ourselves pretty generic, but nothing could be further from the truth.

This particular topic was personally very helpful for me many years ago, when I endeavoured to find my way in the big wide world. I was aware that I had a unique set of fingerprints and my own personal DNA, but one day the magnitude of that awareness resonated with me. I'm not generic in any way: everything about me is unique. I am separate from everyone else on the planet, and their uniqueness is separate from mine.

I know you are acutely aware of your own personal uniqueness; however, be sure to give it enough true introspection. When I did, my world opened up to me; as will yours if you give your own individual uniqueness some consideration.

I realized that day that I'm not just here to take up space. This was enlightening to me on several levels: business, personal, and spiritual. You can spin your uniqueness any way you want to. But the way I spun mine was, *if all this is just an accident, why would all this uniqueness be necessary to me?* Your own interpretation, well: that's up to you.

Nevertheless, once we can accept our personal uniqueness, we get the sense that many things are possible. I can step outside the box; after all, I'm already there—I'm unique already.

Be Patient

Although patience is a virtue, it is not most people's position of strength. Things usually take longer than the time we have allocated for them, so we need to trust in our skills.

Everything in life has an ebb and flow: sometimes we embark

on a quest and, as fortune would have it, we experience the flow, expediting our accomplishment. On the other side of the coin, the ebb presents itself instead, pushing our finish line further away.

If our goal is one of substantial size, we will undoubtedly encounter several ebbs along with multiple flows. We need to be patient and trust in our skills to pull us onwards toward our worthwhile vision.

Living in a state of *Expecting Awesome Daily* is a winding road. There will be rare times when success comes easily; however, experiencing the ups and downs of life is the more common route. A positive mindset is required to push ourselves toward that dream we have set. Patience is at the forefront of a positive mindset.

As we travel down the metaphorical road of success, a lack of patience will leave us broken down at the side of the road. If you don't want to be stranded in the middle of nowhere, be patient and keep your foot on that pedal. Will there be some unexpected detours? Yes, of course there will be; just keep moving in the right direction.

One of my favourite things is a good, old-fashioned road trip: there is so much adventure to be had. On one particular trip, we encountered a bridge that was out. It was unfortunate—not something we'd expected. Our solution was to backtrack about 80km and work our way around.

The possibility of abandoning our trip and heading home wasn't even under consideration. And yet, when people encounter a metaphorical bridge that is out they abandon their quest and head directly back to their comfort zone.

You already possess what you need to manoeuvre around obstacles. Exercise some patience and chart your new course.

Just as an FYI, the opposite of patience is to continually

over-react to every little challenge that litters your path. Be a solution-driven person: if the bridge is out, work your way around it and continue forward. If you have deemed the destination as important, a solution is necessary.

In a Nutshell

To spend our days *Expecting Awesome* events daily, taking stock of the skills we already possess will be mandatory.

The first item we should acknowledge is our uniqueness: the more I ponder this reality, the more impressed I become with life itself. A person who takes the time to acknowledge their personal uniqueness has a reliable weapon against any identity crisis that comes their way.

It's been my observation, with both myself and those I've had an opportunity to coach, that we are a lot closer to our goals than we give ourselves credit for. The place you envision as your destination is a ways down the path for sure: but it probably isn't as far removed as you might have sold yourself on.

The road to success is often a winding one. Be patient, stay focussed, and enjoy some unexpected experiences.

What Do You Have?

Helpful Exercise

I firmly believe that we are a lot more powerful than we give ourselves credit for. We also possess many skills that remain untapped. Make a list of what you perceive as your ten best qualities. Once you itemize them, you can begin the process of developing them. These skills will come in handy in that amazing future you have planned for yourself.

My Ten Best Attributes:
1) _____
2) _____
3) _____
4) _____
5) _____
6) _____
7) _____
8) _____
9) _____
10) _____

You are much further down the path than you realize, and you already possess most of the required skills.

Give yourself credit. You are doing so much better than you think you are. You are so much more accomplished than you know.

Brianna Wiest

Chapter Ten

FIRE UP THE ROCKET

WHEN WE DREAM about our future, we imagine ourselves enjoying life's pleasures in perfect situations. In most cases our dreaming involves being somewhat financially secure. Although this is far from the only goal, it's difficult to picture our perfect future with the stress of money problems. So although we don't dream solely about financial resources, the life we desire will often require financial means.

I would say that it's high time we put an end to the dreaming and start the process of living that dream; it's time for our fantasy to become our reality. It's time to *fire up the rocket*. Chart a course and launch yourself into an amazing future.

It's sad really, that most people live their entire lives sitting on the launch pad. They never get to the step of engaging the launch sequence. We need to take a breath, muster up a massive amount of courage, and give the "all systems go" acknowledgment.

You can live your life in launch-ready position—most do. Maybe life on the metaphorical launch pad isn't all that bad: perhaps you're married, have two children, work a decent job, and enjoy an annual vacation. But in your heart, you are acutely aware that you were made for much more.

I would recommend flipping the ignition as quickly as possible: go ahead and engage that launch sequence. It doesn't change the marriage, two children, or the annual vacation; it just makes everything that much better.

When people dream about what could be, they are, in fact, viewing their perfect future in their mind's eye. That perfect future is of them rocketing around the realm of potential and possibility. Of course, being secure on the launch pad is the safer route in life. However, life is short. Let's get off the launch pad and explore life's possibilities.

This book is about *Expecting Awesome Daily*. I know it would certainly be difficult to expect that level of awesome when locked down on the launch pad. I'm not saying that awesome circumstances won't visit you periodically on the launch pad: for sure they will. But if you desire to live in the expectation that awesome events will occur to you daily, take a breath and give the nod: it's time for adventure.

The decision to either live in launch position or make the call to *fire up the rocket* is totally ours; no one else can make this decision for us. We need to do our part in order to launch ourselves up into the unknown. In fact, this is exactly why most people spend their lives in a state of mediocrity: to avoid that great unknown.

Progressive thinkers, however, are eager for the adventure of the unknown. Successful people ignited that rocket a long time ago: they spend their days whooshing around to obtain all kinds of experiences. Some of these experiences are good ones, while some are bad. But when a bad experience presents itself, these people can't spend much time dwelling on it, because other experiences are occurring. On the launch pad it's a little different: there's lots of time to dwell.

We are designed to dream. Ambition and adventure are built into our DNA. It's the stationary element of sitting on the launch pad that runs against our nature, which explains why we feel so unfulfilled when we remain there.

Do yourself a favour: activate the launch sequence and experience life the way we were designed to. Let go of the comfort zone and fulfill your potential. It's an amazing world, and it's time to experience it instead of viewing it from afar.

You Are Not Created for Mediocrity

Most people have a genuine desire to achieve what they perceive as success. For that reason, it's a good thing we were not designed for mediocrity. Human beings are wired to advance: it's a gift, really. Our purpose, among others, is to be productive. We are meant to spend our days moving in a positive direction: we're not here to simply take up space.

And isn't that convenient? We want to move in a forward direction, and we are hardwired to do exactly that.

Pay close attention to how you feel when your life is stagnant or stuck in a pattern. It doesn't matter if your circumstance is self-inflicted, or if you're experiencing an unwanted challenge through no fault of your own. Either way, as each day stacks upon the previous one, you will become more and more despondent.

It's amazing how quickly we can feel lethargic, unfocussed,

and out of shape. Why is it that we succumb to these feelings so quickly when we're living in a rut? The answer is because we are not operating in a state we are pre-wired to occupy.

I will say that there are some exceptions: when you have achieved a comfortable retirement, for instance, or when you are in a position that finances are no longer a concern. Then, things do change. Your subconscious mind is no longer in forward motion—at least, not in the area of finances.

This creates a level of contentment that is not experienced if your brain is still acutely aware that you need financial security. However, the other aspects of your life will still need attention: they will desire a direction to move toward. This applies to all the aspects of our lives, be it spiritual, family, or friends.

I would think that most people reading this book fall into the category of those looking to create financial security, perhaps in order to facilitate a quality life, retirement, or the ability to help others in need. I realize there are, in fact, quite a few people who simply have no interest in taking their rightful place in society, despite being wired to advance. But I would also assume that they would not have an interest in reading this book.

In our quest to *Expect Awesome Daily*, it's helpful to understand that you are designed to advance. You are driven to move forward from the day you are born to the day you take your last breath. Success would be quite the challenge for us if that were not true.

Fortunately for us, it is true. Despite this, you may still periodically find yourself in a rut; I certainly do. But now you possess the knowledge that life in a rut is not life's natural state: moving forward and continually advancing is.

If you have accidentally found yourself in a rut, regardless of where the fault lies, make a decision today to get yourself out of it. Move past your current challenge and live your life the way it was intended, by continually moving forward and exploring new experiences. Humans desire to advance; you are not exempt from the process.

The World Depends on You

This statement may seem a little dramatic to you. Or perhaps it doesn't. Maybe you were made for great things on a world-proportioned stage. Or maybe your contribution is closer to home, among your friends, family, and those geographically accessible to you. Neither is more significant or less: your responsibility is to do your part and fill the gap where you're needed.

Do not make the common mistake of underestimating your abilities. Doing so will limit your effectiveness at being the person you are compelled to be. You possess immense power: so much so that this chapter's analogy of a rocket may be an underestimate. You possess a level of potential far beyond your current reality; you can affect the world in a massive way.

I can't say if the change you can effect is on a global scale or an equally-important level closer to home. I can, however, say unequivocally that the possibility for change resides within you. Your job is to get it from inside you to those who need it. The world is depending on you, and the ball is in your court. It's time! *Fire up the rocket.*

Obstacles Make Us Stronger

We tend to say that obstacles make us stronger when we're encouraging someone who is battling a challenge. I think we say it because, in most cases, we don't really know what else to say.

However, that doesn't change the fact that we're sharing a truth.

If you want to have bigger muscles, you can't simply repeat affirmations to yourself until you get more impressive biceps. The process requires time and commitment to curl those weights. Your muscles consider the weights an obstacle: no obstacle, no gain. It's as simple as that.

Life works the exact same way; if we want to have progression, we must have resistance. Unfortunately, most people search for a path that offers the least resistance to success. That would be like joining a gym to get a better body, and then desperately avoiding that gym at all costs. I realize it sounds crazy, but that is exactly what most people do.

Our ability to *Expect Awesome Daily* should be full of necessary obstacles. We should spend our days searching for personal growth opportunities (AKA obstacles) as opposed to avoiding them.

If you go fishing, it makes sense to fish where the fish are. You could use all your fishing skills and techniques, but if the fish are not there, your efforts will be in vain. We must fish where the fish are.

Sometimes, life will grant you an achievement without anything you perceive as an obstacle. When that happens, take it and be happy. However, I must tell you that is not how it goes most of the time. I should also point out that you shouldn't want success without hurdles, since that's where the growth happens.

The sooner you accept the fact that obstacles are a part of the personal growth puzzle, the better off you will be.

Don't Just Dream: Go Where the Rocket Takes You

For many, I would say it's high time to stop dreaming. Instead, activate that launch sequence: 3, 2, 1, it's time to go.

If you're being honest with yourself, you'll admit that you have been spending way too much time on the launch pad. In fact, you've likely spent so much time there it has begun to feel like home, and spending your life in the launch-ready position has become the norm.

I realize for some people this is not the truth—yet. But I can assure you that if you do not purposefully *fire up the rocket*, this launch pad may not become home, but it sure will feel like it.

Although a number of people consciously launch themselves toward their dreams, a much larger group never leave the comfort zone of their launch pad. In truth, they have probably never even realized they were made for greater things. Their lives, albeit probably quite happy, are absent of the mental reaching for what could be.

This chapter is not intended in any way to discount their lives. That's the choice they made, and that's good with me! Most of my friends and relatives fall into this large percentage of our society. Live your life, contribute, and be happy.

My reference here is for those that possess a *bona fide* inner desire to be greater. That's not everyone, and that's fine. However, if it's you, then quickly activate the launch sequence; the longer you linger, the greater the odds that the launch pad will be your final destination.

Since you are reading this book, odds are you fall into the category of those desiring to launch. Once you know where you want to go, don't hesitate—I know you've made that procrastination mistake in the past. Activate the launch sequence and let's get going.

The world of opportunity is an amazing place: it may not be unlimited, but it sure feels like it is. So spend your days rocketing around, exploring amazing places, meeting interesting people, and discovering new opportunities.

You probably found the launch pad a long time ago. For sure there is some excitement to be had there, dreaming about what could be. But it will never be real until you engage that launch sequence and hold on tight.

Someday, we will all breathe our last and leave this world. I have my beliefs, as do you, about what plays out after that. None of us can say for certain when that transition will occur; it may be soon, or perhaps quite a ways down the road. The point is, for now we live in the physical world, and someday we won't be. So for now, I recommend you take full advantage of your situation: go where the rocket will take you.

I should mention that this metaphorical rocket isn't a guided tour: you are the pilot. You decide when to fire it up, and you have the wheel. You have to know where you want to go. If you don't, then you haven't even found the launch pad yet.

It's time to stop fantasizing about where we want this life to take us and just begin the journey. You have procrastinated enough for several lifetimes. *Fire up the rocket* and launch yourself into your amazing future: a future that lives *Expecting Awesome Daily*.

In a Nutshell

We all want to live on the lookout for amazing and exciting adventures daily. So it's time we fired up the rocket and launched ourselves into exactly that.

Although many do choose a mediocre lifestyle, we are not designed for it. There are others around you who are in need of what you can do, and can benefit from what you will discover.

I'm not saying you can change the world, but I'm equally not saying that you cannot. I can say that we all need to do our part: for some, that is on a grand scale, while for others it is closer to home. Either way, *fire up the rocket* and see how far you can go.

When life is over and others reflect upon you, their clear and honest opinion should be that was a life well-lived.

I hope you've found my advice helpful. These thoughts are where the personal rocket that I'm strapped to take me. I trust your own rocket will take you to many amazing places and experiences. You are an amazing person: please accept that!

Life is like riding a bicycle. To keep your balance, you must keep moving.

Albert Einstein

FINAL THOUGHTS

I FEEL IT is now important that I reiterate my opening point: this book, albeit beneficial to your daily attitude, is in no way the most important aspect of your life. For each person, that aspect is different: for instance, for me, my spiritual position is what occupies that position. It's important that you spend some time examining what the most important aspect is for you.

Assuming you take my advice, you can spend whatever days are allotted to you in an optimal state of mind. If you are going to be here for a while anyway, you might as well maximize. If we don't purposefully *Expect Awesome Daily*, we will automatically fall into life's opposite mode of thinking: filling our days with a constant state of worry.

As a business coach, I am often asked how to get over continuous stressful thinking. By now, you should know the answer to this all-too common question: live your days in a constant state of *Expecting Awesome Daily*. When you flip a light switch, all the darkness flees from the room; that is exactly what happens to worry and stress when you flip the switch of *Expecting Awesome Daily*.

None of the books I write will add days to your life or help you in whatever comes after; that is not my intention. What I am sincerely interested in is making your life better while you are still here: that's my goal. And since I know there are many books for you to read on this subject, I sincerely appreciate you taking the time to read my thoughts on it.

Thank you and God bless! Have an awesome life.

NOTES